The BOYHOOD *and* YOUTH *of*

Napoleon

Corsica

0 ____ 10 ____ 20 miles
0 __ 10 __ 20 __ 30 km

CAP CORSE

Bastia

L'Ile Rousse

Saint Florent
Furiani

Calvi
Algajola

Murato
Borgo

Ponte Novo

NIOLO
Golo

ROSTINO

CASINCA

Soveria

Lozzi

Corte

Restonica

Monte Rotondo

Tavignano

Bocognano

Col de Vizzavona

Liamone

Gravona

Aleria

TALAVO

Ajaccio

Zicavo

Taravo

TALLANO

Sollacaro

Ste Lucie
de Tallano

Sartene

Porto
Vecchio

Bonifacio

The BOYHOOD and YOUTH of

Napoleon

NAPOLEON BONAPARTE 1769-1793

OSCAR BROWNING

FONTHILL

Fonthill Media Limited
Fonthill Media LLC
www.fonthillmedia.com
office@fonthillmedia.com

This edition published in the United Kingdom 2012

British Library Cataloguing in Publication Data:
A catalogue record for this book is available from the British Library

ISBN 978-1-78155-011-3 (print)
ISBN 978-1-78155-155-4 (e-book)

Typeset in 11pt on 14pt Sabon.
Printed and bound in England

Connect with us
 facebook.com/fonthillmedia   twitter.com/fonthillmedia

Contents

	Introduction to the 2012 Edition	7
I	Birth and Childhood	13
II	Brienne	20
III	Departure for Paris	27
IV	The École Militaire de Paris	34
V	Valence and Auxonne	43
VI	Corsica	54
VII	Auxonne and Valence	61
VIII	Ajaccio	72
IX	Paris	84
X	La Maddalena	90
XI	Paoli	95
XII	Le Souper de Beaucaire	108
XIII	Toulon	113
	Appendix I	126
	Appendix II	139
	Appendix III	141
	Appendix IV	148

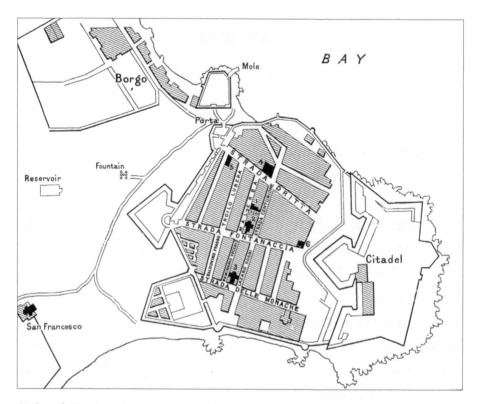

A plan of Ajaccio, 1769.
1 Casa (the house of) the Bonaparte family
2 Oratorio di San Giovanni Battista
3 Duomo
4 Casa Pozzo di Borgo
5 Casa Peraldi
6 Casa Ramolini

Introduction to
the 2012 Edition

The Boyhood and Youth of Napoleon is an interesting and well written book, based on credible sources, by a lecturer of distinction, even if his colourful life (for the times) was unacceptable in college circles. In fact, in terms of colour there were few to beat Oscar Browning.

Oscar Browning, (1837-1923), was born in London, third son of William Shipton Browning, a distiller, of Smithfield. He attended a boarding-school in the late 1840s and was then tutored for two years (1848-50) by his brother, a curate. In 1851 he was sent to Eton College, where he was unpopular and ill-treated and found life there to be coarse, brutal, dirty, and unloving. The food was so meagre that he nearly starved. When later he was a housemaster he ensured that the atmosphere of his house was high-minded, affectionate, and urbane. At Eton he became infatuated with a fellow pupil called Dunmore, and from that point on, snobbery and homosexuality were entrenched for life.

In 1856 Browning was elected to a scholarship at King's College, Cambridge. Three years later he was elected to a fellowship, which, as he never married, by prevailing college regulations he retained until his death. Ostracized by his fellow Etonians at King's for speaking at the union, he befriended men at Trinity, where he found an intellectual set in which strong affections were sublimated into high educational ideals.

In 1860 Browning accepted the position of assistant mastership at Eton, where he ran a boarding-house from 1862. This house was presided over by his beautiful, dignified, and accomplished mother, soon to become the most popular in the school. This generated a large income which Browning spent in the interests of the boys. His house had a controversially Pre-Raphaelite tone; the food was nourishing and plentiful, the curtains were by William Morris, the noted and eccentric designer. There was much jolliness, but the bronzes and marbles in his corridors discouraged rough-housing. Though he participated in many sports he detested the cult of athleticism. His history lessons were highly successful, but shocked the headmaster, who thought that both Queen Anne and the French Revolution were dangerous subjects for study. Oscar Browning—OB as he came to be called—passionately desired to reform Eton so that it could educate an effective governing class for a democratic age. To foster this élite, he urged reform of the curriculum to emphasize modern history and foreign languages and to minimize science and mathematics. His proposed reforms would have ensured for him luxurious living and unbounded intimacy with favourite boys, but were resisted by the forces of staid inanition. Many of his colleagues were pompous, small-minded, and vindictive, and he showed them much rancour. Meanwhile he cultivated intelligent boys and went abroad every school vacation, travelling in princely style with a courier, usually to Italy and often accompanied by an Eton boy. He encouraged sexual confidences, and despite his own erotic fantasies, took a strong purifying line against masturbation and spooning. His intimate, indiscreet friendship with a boy in another boarding-house, G. N. Curzon—later the politician and viceroy—provoked a crisis and amid national controversy he was dismissed in 1875 on the pretext of administrative inefficiency but actually because his influence was thought to be sexually contagious. The boys, their parents, and his friends rallied indignantly but vainly around him, and the matter was widely canvassed in the press and the clubs of London, and even debated in the House of Commons, but the Eton headmaster refused to budge. As a result Browning found his income of £3,000 taken away and he had to fall back on the income from his fellowship of £300 per annum.

The innuendoes from Eton left a residual odium, and some senior members of King's were dismayed by OB's return as a resident fellow. Nevertheless, he helped to expand the college. He did good work in promoting King's to higher intellectual standards: the nascent historical tripos received his eager support, and he was an innovative tutor, requiring a weekly essay from his history pupils. He hoped to remodel King's to emulate Balliol or the École Normale in Paris.

OB obtained a college lectureship at King's in 1880 and a university lectureship in 1884. As part of his professional rehabilitation he became a fellow of the Royal Historical Society and the chairman of its council in 1885. He was, in 1885, the first professional historian to contribute to its *Transactions*, with papers on the triple alliance of 1788 and the Anglo-French commercial treaty of 1786. For the society's Camden Series he transcribed and annotated *The Political Memoranda of Francis, Fifth Duke of Leeds*, 1774-1796, and two volumes of the third duke of Dorset's diplomatic dispatches from Paris from 1784 to 1790. The focus of his historical interests on high politics and foreign affairs indicated that, despite his role in the professionalization of history teaching, he regarded history as a tool in training statesmen, and himself as a professional educator rather than a professional historian.

OB was a keen radical, though with a tinge of imperialism. Three times he contested hopeless seats before finally giving up on politics. He travelled constantly, even when old, and maintained an extensive correspondence with a polished horde of celebrities. He had an attractive mixture of the high-spirited and self-important. He was the only man to have sung with the future Queen Mary 'The Man who Broke the Bank at Monte Carlo', accompanied by a barrel organ. He also declared that, when faced with a hard decision, he asked himself what Napoleon would have done in his place.

OB was popular with undergraduates and he made himself the centre of a set where his smallest gestures were magnified into significance and he became a tremendous Cambridge personality. His eccentricities enabled his protégés to share emotional intimacy without impermissible sexual contact. One reminiscence depicted one of OB's 'at homes', on a Sunday evening, as a convivial gathering of undergraduates, metaphysicians, and peers at which no one thought it strange that there was 'a Tommy in scarlet uniform' playing the clarinet or that when OB finished 'trolling out *Voi che sapete* with immense gusto' on the piano 'the clarinet-player gave him a spanking'. His friendships were never intense or soulful but cheerful affairs with young sailors, artisans, and stable-lads to whom he was kind and hospitable. He was generous and romantic with perpetual hope of finding a mute, inglorious Milton: a shopboy in Hastings who impressed him as a genius was one of many grateful youths whom he employed as a secretary.

OB's conversation was ample, and for many years witty, but with increasing age his anecdotage became offensively self-centred. He had prodigious vitality and magnificent *élan*. His admirers found him affectionate, generous, lavish of money, self-mocking, Rabelaisian, and impulsive. He was very gifted and Polish was his fortieth language; others were Yiddish and Esperanto. OB always adored music, notably Mozart, and attended the first Bayreuth performance of Wagner's Ring cycle.

Browning's years at King's from 1905 were especially acrimonious as his enforced retirement became imminent. In 1909 he was forcibly superannuated from his lectureship. OB moved to Rome where he lived at Palazzo Simonetti, via Pietro Cavallini 12, spending some time giving public lectures. He remained there until his death.

Browning indulged himself in his interests and his amusements, and yet he worked hard and was sincere in his educational motives. Clearly he had a deep interest in Napoleon, a subject he returned to time and time again, and he saw from his long study on his topic that Napoleon had a genius for government. *The Boyhood and Youth of Napoleon* is one of his last publications, and one to which he had given much thought over a period of many years. The popular topic of Napoleon had suffered much from hack writers for over a century, where a wealth of published material made the quarrying work relatively easy. OB did not fall into this trap and his professional training, his discerning understanding of intelligent boys and young men, and the use of Napoleon's own writings mixed with reliable source material allowed him to see his subject very clearly. His linguistic skills enabled him to read many documents and books in their original languages and he synthesized his many sources to produce a short, but readable portrait of the young hero. In particular he read Bourienne with caution, and avoided the pitfalls of accepting sources at their literal face-value. In doing this, he has left us with a well-considered biography which has not lost any value in the hundred years since its first publication.

This short introduction his based to an extensive degree on the interesting and much fuller entry provided in the *Dictionary of National Biography*.

PREFACE

During the Hundred Days, there lay in Napoleon's study in the Tuileries a packet of papers, sealed with the Imperial arms, on the cover of which was written, "À remettre au Cardinal Fesch seul." This packet was carried by Fesch to Rome, but he never had the curiosity to open it, and it remained sealed and tied up till his death, on May 13th, 1839. After this event, it was carried, with many other papers, to Lyons by the Abbé Lyonnet, his Vicar-General, who wrote his life. In the following year, Prince Charles-Lucien, the eldest son of Lucien Bonaparte, opened the packet, but failed to recognize the importance of the papers. He did not therefore claim them for the family, and they remained in the possession of Lyonnet. He was hesitating whether he should present them to some library, or sell them for the benefit of the poor, when William Libri, the well-known collector, who had heard of their existence, succeeded in purchasing them for about £300. Libri eventually sold the manuscripts to Lord Ashburnham, but it is only too probable that before this was done he had disposed of fragments of the collection to other persons. Some of these papers were published by Libri in the *Revue des Deux Mondes*, and in *L'Illustration*. In 1881, Prince Napoleon became aware of the existence of these documents. By the kindness of Lord Ashburnham they were deposited for some days in the British Museum, in order that they might be examined, and a catalogue of them was made by M. Masson, together with a transcript of the most important papers.

When the Ashburnham collection was sold in 1884, the papers passed into the hands of the Italian Government, and they were deposited in the Laurentian Library at Florence, where they are still to be seen. Here they came under the charge of Signor Biagi, the Director of the Library, who intended to publish them, and had them carefully copied, and in 1895 they were published by MM. Masson and Biagi, in a book entitled *Napoleon*

Inconnu. M. Masson added to the manuscripts some notes on the early life of Napoleon, drawn from other papers, which were either in the Libri packet, or which came into his hands from other sources, especially from Corsican families connected with Napoleon's youth. They included some valuable documents which had been left in the Napoleon house at Ajaccio by Madame Mère, concealed under a heap of coal by M. Levie-Landino, and exposed to the ravages of damp and rats.

M. Arthur Chuquet, well known for his admirable history of the wars of the Revolution, has consecrated three volumes to the life of Napoleon, from his birth to the siege of Toulon. He bases his work on the writings of Jung, Du Teil, and Coston, but above all on the documents of Masson, the knowledge of which is indispensable to the proper understanding of the subject. But M. Chuquet has done much more than this. With unrivalled industry and acuteness he has got together a number of facts about Corsica, about the condition of the military schools of France, and especially about those in which the young Napoleon was educated, which throw a flood of light on the situation. He depicts for us, not only Napoleon as he was in his childhood, boyhood, and youth, but invests him with an atmosphere which makes us almost as familiar with him as if we had been his contemporaries. These two works, the *Napoleon Inconnu* of Masson and *La Jeunesse de Napoleon* of Chuquet, furnish us with all the information necessary for an adequate understanding of Napoleon's youth. But I have not stopped at this, and there is no book contained in the admirable bibliography of Kircheisen, which bears on this period, which I have not examined so far as was necessary for my purpose. At the same time, I have kept in view that I am not writing a History of France, or of Europe between the years 1769 and 1793, but only a personal account of Napoleon during this period. The end result is to place the character of Napoleon in a more favourable, or I may say, in a more human, light.

CHAPTER I

BIRTH AND CHILDHOOD

Napoleon Bonaparte was born at Ajaccio on 15 August 1769, the son of Charles-Marie de Bonaparte and of Marie-Letizia Ramolino. The family of Bonaparte was probably of Tuscan origin, and was originally settled at Florence. In the eleventh century a branch of the family established itself at San Miniato, where a Canon Filippo Buonaparte was living in the last years of the eighteenth century. Charles Bonaparte visited this distant cousin when he went to take his degree of Doctor of Laws at the University of Pisa, and Napoleon slept at his house on 29 June 1796. Another branch of the same family was established at Sarzana, a city well known to the students of Dante. From this place Francesco Buonaparte removed to Corsica, in the year 1529. He was the direct ancestor of Napoleon. The family lived at Ajaccio, but their principal possessions were at Bocognano and Bastelica, at a considerable distance from the capital.

Napoleon's father was a handsome, courtly gentleman of unusual culture and distinguished manners. He was generally in want of money, and showed considerable ingenuity and address in obtaining the assistance which he needed. On 2 June 1764, at the age of eighteen, he married Letizia Ramolino, four years younger than himself, a girl of singular beauty. She belonged, like her husband, to a Florentine family, which settled in Corsica at the end of the fifteenth century; indeed, in Corsica, her family is regarded as superior to that of the Bonapartes. Her father died when she was five years old, and two years afterwards her mother married a Captain Fesch, of Swiss origin. From this union was born, in 1763, an only son, Joseph Fesch, afterwards Cardinal, who was therefore Napoleon's uncle, but only six years older than himself.

Madame Mère, as she was afterwards called, preserved her good looks and her youthful appearance till old age. She was full of courage and spirits, and followed her husband through woods and mountains in the last days of Corsican independence. She was devoted to her children, but brought them up with severity. Many tales are told of her chastisement of Napoleon. Once, when he was nearly grown up, he laughed at his grandmother, and called her an old witch. Letizia was very angry, and Napoleon, knowing that he would be punished, kept out of her way. However, going to his bedroom to dress for dinner, she followed him, and taking advantage of his deshabille, gave him a good thrashing. Napoleon derived from his mother many of his strongest qualities, among others his habit of economy. The devotion between mother and son, which lasted throughout their lives, is one of the most beautiful episodes in modern history. Charles Bonaparte lost his father at the age of fourteen, and was brought up under the fostering care of his uncle Lucien, Archdeacon of the Cathedral of Ajaccio. He was devoted to the cause of Paoli, served as his aide-de-camp, and was regarded by some as his probable successor; indeed, his marriage with Letizia could not have been arranged without the intervention of Paoli.

When the war broke out, the Bonapartes declared emphatically against France. The proclamation addressed to the youth of Corsica, in favour of independence, was the composition of Charles Bonaparte. Napoleon was proud of it, and quoted some of it from memory at St Helena. When the Corsican patriots were defeated at Ponte Nuovo, the Bonapartes had to take refuge in the maquis, and Letizia accompanied her husband through the brushwood and across the bridgeless rivers with Joseph in her arms and Napoleon in her womb. Eventually Charles saw that resistance was hopeless, and that the wisest course was to give in to the French. He also hoped to obtain a place under government. In fact, in February, 1771, he was appointed assessor of the Royal Jurisdiction of Ajaccio, one of the eleven jurisdictions into which the island was then divided, his duty being to assist the judge, both in civil and criminal affairs, and to take his place when he was absent. Charles, we must remember, had previously taken the degree of Doctor of Laws in the University of Pisa. From this moment he became a devoted Royalist, and paid court to the two French commissioners, Marbœuf and Boucheporn.

In June, 1777, Charles Bonaparte was elected deputy of the nobility, to represent the interests of Corsica at Versailles. He went to France at the close of 1778, and returned in the spring of 1779. His devotion to Marbœuf was well repaid. Marbœuf became godfather to his son Louis (named after the King), he placed Napoleon at the military school of Brienne, sent Marianna to St Cyr, and Fesch to the Seminary of Aix. He assisted him also in many other ways.

As has been said above, Napoleon was born at Ajaccio, on 15 August 1769, the Feast of the Assumption of the Virgin. His mother was on her way to the mid-day Mass when she was seized with the pains of labour and could not reach her bedroom. It is said that the child entered the world with a great noise, as if he wished to take possession of it. The name Napoleon is rare, but not unknown. Napoleon's great-grandfather had, in the early part of the eighteenth century, called his three sons Joseph, Napoleon, and Lucien, and Napoleon's father determined to follow his example. When Napoleon became Consul he conceived a disgust for the name, but this passed away, and he eventually recognized its power. It has been said that he was really the eldest son, and that he was born in 1768, but careful examination of the evidence shows this to be a mistake. Letizia's eldest child, a boy, was born in 1765, and died in 1768. According to the determination above mentioned, he bore the name of Joseph, and Joseph, who was born just before he died, was at first called Nabulione. But on the death of the first-born, Joseph was inserted before Nabulione in the register, as being the name of the eldest of the family, whilst the child born in 1769 received the name of Napoleon, and no other. The whole family regarded Joseph as the eldest son, although Napoleon was, in fact, the head of it.

In a document written before 1789, called "Epochs of My Life," Napoleon states that he was born 15 August 1769, and the certificate of Napoleon's baptism still exists. It is signed by the godfather, the godmother, and the father of the child, and by the clerk of the parish of Ajaccio, Diamante. It is dated 21 July 1771, and states that in the paternal house, by permission of the Reverend Lucien Bonaparte, the holy ceremonies and prayers have been administered to Napoleon, born 15 August 1769.

The nearest relations of the young Napoleon were, in the first place, his father's mother, Maria Saveria Bonaparte, generally called Minanna Saveria, who lived and died in the Napoleon house in the Rue St Charles. She was on excellent terms with Letizia, whose only complaint was that she spoiled the children. Besides this, there was his mother's sister, Gertrude Paravicini, whom he called "Zia Gertrude" (Aunt Gertrude), and his mother's aunt, Marianna Pietra Santa, whose daughter married an Arrighi.

Before we enter upon a narrative of Napoleon's life, it will be well to give some account of the condition of Corsica at this time. Corsica had belonged to Genoa, but, exasperated by bad government, had risen in rebellion, and was endeavouring to achieve her independence under the leadership of Paoli. In 1764 Genoa, reduced to extremities and despairing of being able to preserve the few fortresses left to her in the island, or to save the garrisons which were imprisoned in their citadels by Paoli, asked for assistance from Louis XV. France, at this time, owed Genoa several millions, and it was agreed that the debt should be paid by French troops being allowed to garrison the fortresses for four years. When this arrangement came to an end in 1768, Genoa ceded Corsica to France. Paoli protested that Genoa had no right to dispose of the Corsicans as if they were cattle, but no attention was paid to him. Paoli still held out, but was defeated on 9 May 1769, in the battle of Ponte Nuovo. He left the island on 12 June and took refuge first in Tuscany and then in England.

Corsica thus became French in 1769, but the acquisition of the island was not popular in France, and many were of opinion that it would be better if it could be once for all submerged in the Mediterranean. Choiseul and others argued that if Corsica were of little use to France, it would be disastrous to expose it to the power of her enemies. Any enemy in possession of Corsica could intercept the communications of France with Spain, Italy, and the Levant, so that the coasts of Provence and Languedoc would be exposed to attack. On the other hand, it secured to its possessors the command of the Mediterranean.

Corsica was governed by two commissioners, appointed by the King, one styled the governor, the other the intendant, one military, the other civil. The governors at this period were Marbœuf, 1772-1786, and Barrin, 1786-1790. The best known of the intendants was Boucheporn, who held office for ten years, from 1775-1785, and was known as the Grand Vizir of Marbœuf. The judicial administration of the island was committed to a Conseil Superieur, which was a kind of parliament, and to a number of royal jurisdictions. The Conseil Superieur, created in 1768, sat at Bastia, and consisted of a first and second president, ten councillors, of whom six were French and four Corsican, a French procureur-général and his substitute, a greffier, and two secretaryinterpreters. The governor had the privilege of sitting in this parliament, and had a deliberative voice. Each jurisdiction contained a judge-royal, an assessor, a procureur du roi, and a greffier. The first three officers were always appointed in ratio of two Corsicans to one Frenchman.

The civil government of the island, organized in 1771, was on this wise. First came the *paese*, or village, governed by a Podestà, and two Fathers of the village elected by heads of families over twenty-five years of age; then the *pieve*, or canton, governed by a Podestà Maggiore, elected every year from the most considerable personages of the *pieve*; then the province, at the head of which was an inspector of noble rank, appointed by the king.

Corsica was constituted as a *pays d'état*, with three orders—clergy, nobles, and *tiers état*. The Estates met at Bastia, each order having twenty-three deputies. The deputies of the clergy were the five bishops of the island, who might be represented by their vicars-general, and eighteen *pievani*, or deans, elected by the assemblies of the ten provinces, monks being excluded. At the close of each session the Estates nominated a permanent commission of twelve nobles, called the Nobili Dodici, and it was arranged that a member of the twelve should always be attached to the suite of the Royal Commissioners.

Nobility had not been recognized in Corsica before the French occupation, as the Genoese had done everything in their power to debase the Corsican aristocracy. They had deprived them of education, had kept them out of high office, and had forbidden them to engage in commerce, for fear they should become rich. There was, therefore, little difference in Corsica between the manner of dress and of life of nobles and peasants. The new French Government pursued a different policy. They set themselves to develop and foster a class of men who could be attached to the government by interest, and would prove a counterpoise to the clergy and the *tiers état*. They therefore established a nobility, accepting as proof such titles as could be got together. The Bonapartes were assisted in this research by the Grand Duke of Tuscany and by the Archbishop of Pisa. They bore a count's coronet, and their arms were gules, two bars azure, between two stars of the second, and the letters B.P. As we have said, the twelve nobles and the ten inspectors of provinces were drawn entirely from the nobility, while the children of noble families were admitted gratuitously to the College Mazarin, the Seminary of Aix, to the royal military schools, and to the ladies' college of St Cyr. Marbœuf did his best to inspire the somewhat uncultivated Corsicans with French refinement. They began to adopt French fashions of dress, but the effect was somewhat ludicrous at first. Before this the children used to walk about with bare feet, and the girls used to fetch water from the fountain and carry it home on their heads. Besides this, Corsicans were admitted into every regiment of the army, and a special Corsican regiment was formed—the Royal-Corse. The Corsicans paid but few taxes. Indeed, the island was a burden to the Exchequer, and did not pay its expenses by the sum of 600,000 livres a year.

Still the islanders were discontented, and regretted their loss of liberty. A general once said to a peasant, "In the days of your Paoli you paid double what you do now." "Yes," replied the peasant; "but then we gave, now you take." The flag of Corsica was argent, a Moor's head proper,

17

bandaged over the eyes. It was forbidden by the French, but was used by the islanders whenever they found a chance.

Peace was maintained in Corsica, but only by a system of terror. The possession of guns was forbidden, as was also the sale of stiletti, but there was great difficulty in putting down assassination. Corsica was at first governed by the War Office. In 1773 it was made over to the Abbé Terray to farm the taxes, as controlleur-general; before the Revolution it was restored to the War Office. But it always remained a prey to financiers, fed upon by Frenchmen, and despoiled by a bureaucracy. It felt itself oppressed, and was disaffected. Indeed, the faults of the government gave only too much reason for this disloyalty.

The accounts of Napoleon's infancy have been garnished by a number of stories which are entirely devoid of foundation. The most trustworthy narrative is derived from his mother. She only kept a single servant. The first of these was Mammuccia-Caterina, who received Napoleon when he came into the world. She is said to have been noisy and obstinate, always at loggerheads with the grandmother, although she was very fond of her. She had special charge of the children. Next came the devoted Saveria, whom Joseph brought from Tuscany. She accompanied Madame Letizia everywhere, grew old with her, and died in her house in 1825. In 1813 Napoleon gave her a pension of 1200 francs. Still more important was Napoleon's wet-nurse, Camilla Ilari, wife of a sailor of Ajaccio. She worshipped her foster-child. When Napoleon anchored in the bay of Ajaccio, on his return from Egypt, he perceived in the crowd a woman clothed in black, who cried out, "Caro figlio!" He replied, "Madre." When he disembarked she said to him, "My son, I gave you the milk of my heart; I can now only offer you the milk of my goat;" and she held out a bottle to him. He never forgot her. She was present at his coronation, and was presented to the Pope, who gave her his blessing, and to Josephine, who gave her diamonds. She talked with the Pope for an hour and a half in the Corsican dialect. Napoleon said, "Poor Pope! He must have plenty of time on his hands." He conferred benefits on her and her family, and once presented her granddaughter to the ladies of the court at the Tuileries, saying, "This is my foster-niece, ladies. Never say again that there are not pretty women in Corsica." Her husband, Poli, clung to Napoleon to the last, and did not make his submission to the English till May, 1816.

Napoleon's mother tells us that she had arranged a large empty room for the children to play in. While the others were jumping about, drawing and scribbling on the walls, Napoleon used to beat a drum, wield a sabre of wood, and draw soldiers on the walls ranged in order of battle. He was very industrious, and showed a great capacity for mathematics. His first teachers were nuns. They were very fond of him, and called him the mathematician. He then went to the school which formerly belonged to the Jesuits. He exchanged every day the piece of white bread given him for lunch for the rough brown bread of the common soldier, in order that he might accustom himself to soldiers' fare. At the age of eight he had such a passion for arithmetic that a shed was built for him behind the house, where he might work undisturbed. Sunk in meditation, he walked about in the evening with his stockings about his heels, and was much jeered at in consequence. Letizia has told us that on 5 May 1777, the family bailiff brought to their house two young and spirited horses. Napoleon mounted one of them, and, to the terror of everyone, galloped off to the farm, laughing at their fright. Before he returned he examined the mechanism of the mill carefully, asking how much corn it could grind in an hour, and, on being told, calculated that it could grind so much in a day, and so much in a week. When the farmer brought the child back, he told his mother that, if he lived, he would become the foremost man in the world. Genius, industry, and the power of inspiring and feeling deep affection were the chief notes of Napoleon's early childhood.

At the same time traces of an imperious disposition were not wanting. Napoleon confessed that at this time he was turbulent, aggressive, and quarrelsome. He was afraid of no one, but bit and scratched without reference to inequality of size and age. Joseph, although the elder, was no match for him. The two boys went together at a later period, to a school kept by an Abbé Recco, to whom Napoleon left 20,000 francs in his will. Here the boys, according to the present custom of some Jesuit schools, were arranged on benches opposite each other, under the names of Romans and Carthaginians. To encourage emulation, the walls were hung with swords, shields, spears, and standards made of wood or pasteboard, and the division which was superior in work carried off a trophy from the other. Joseph, as the elder, was classed as a Roman; but Napoleon, who did not like to be a Carthaginian, persuaded him to change places, which he good-naturedly assented to.

CHAPTER II

BRIENNE

Charles Bonaparte determined to make Joseph a priest and Napoleon a soldier. Marbœuf promised to give the latter a scholarship in one of the Royal Military Schools, and to procure for the former an ecclesiastical benefice by means of his nephew, the Bishop of Autun. He proposed to place both of them at the College of Autun, then one of the best public schools in France, which has sometimes been called the French Eton. Joseph was to study classics, and Napoleon to remain a short time to learn French. On 15 December 1778, the father left Ajaccio with his two little boys, one aged nine and the other ten. He also had with him Fesch, his brother-in-law, aged fifteen, who was intending to complete his studies at the Seminary of Aix, and his cousin, Aurelio Varese, who had been appointed sub-deacon to the bishop of Autun. They reached Autun, as Napoleon tells us in his notes, on 1 January 1779. The two brothers were placed under the care of the Abbé de Chardon, who, in 1823, wrote his impressions to a friend. He says, "Napoleon arrived at Autun with his brother Joseph at the commencement of the year 1779, accompanied by his father (who, as you perhaps remember, was a very handsome man), and the Abbé de Varese, who afterwards became Grand Vicar of Autun, doubtless to his own great astonishment, and at a later period married, and was made Commissioner of War."

Joseph was thought to be a good boy, shy, quiet, without ambition. Napoleon, on the other hand, was pensive and sombre, taking no part in games, and walking about alone, which is not unnatural, as he could not speak French. He fired up at the mention of Corsica, and said that if the French had been only four to one, they would never have had Corsica; but they were ten to one. He was cleverer than Joseph, and learned with greater facility. Chardon tells us that in three months he learned sufficient French to converse fluently, and to write little exercises, If Chardon told him anything, he would listen with his eyes and mouth open, and if the same thing were repeated, he did not attend, and when rebuked said, "Sir, I know that already."

Whilst Napoleon was at Autun, his father was completing the arrangements for entering him at one of the military schools. For this two things were necessary—a certificate of nobility for four generations, and a certificate of poverty. About the first there was no difficulty, as the Bonapartes could show eleven generations of nobility, and Charles was about to appear before the King at Versailles as the representative of the nobility of Corsica. For the second, four Corsicans certified that Charles, although noble, had no fortune except his pay as assessor, and could not give his children the education suited to their rank. Hozier de Serigny, the King's genealogist and historiographer, asked Charles some questions, which were answered as follows: that Ramolino was the family name of his wife; that his own name was Charles-Marie; that he used the particule *de*, but that it was generally omitted in Italy; that he wrote his name Buonaparte; and that the name Napoleon, which was Italian, could not be translated into French. Napoleon remained at Autun three months. The register of the college has this entry: "M. Neapoleonne de Buonaparte pour trois mois vingt jours cent onze livres, douze sols, huit deniers, 111*l.* 12*s.* 8*d.*"

In consequence of the efforts of his father, Napoleon was appointed by the War Office, in January, to the royal military school of Tiron, in le Perche, but for some reason of which we are ignorant this arrangement was changed, and he was sent to Brienne. He left Autun on 23 April, taking leave of his brother, who was to remain there five years longer. They loved each other dearly, and Joseph was in tears, while Napoleon shed only one tear, which he endeavoured to conceal. The Abbé Simon, the sub-principal, who was present, said to Joseph, "Your brother has shed only one tear, but that shows his sorrow at leaving you as much as all yours." Here there is a discrepancy in the dates. Napoleon, in his notes, says that he left for Brienne on 12 May, whereas we know that he left Autun on 23 April. It is probable that he spent the intervening time with M. de Champeaux, at his country house of Thoisy-le-Désert, but the matter is of no great importance.

The military schools, of which Brienne was one, were founded by Louis XVI, on the advice of St Germain, Minister of War, in 1776, so that they were now only three years old. They were twelve in number, and, strangely enough, were all administered by religious orders. The Benedictines had Sorèze, Tiron, and four others; the Oratorians, Tournon and three others;

the Regular Canons of the Saviour administered the school of Pont-à-Mousson, and the Minims that of Brienne. Each of these establishments had from fifty to sixty of the poor nobility, receiving a free education at the cost of the king. For each pupil a yearly sum of about £28 was paid by quarterly instalments in advance. For this sum the monks undertook to give each pupil a separate room or cell, to place them in a building apart, to feed and clothe them, to teach them writing, French, Latin, German, history and geography, mathematics, drawing, music, dancing, and fencing. As it was part of the plan of St Germain that these young nobles should not be educated by themselves, the monks were to receive at least an equal number of pensioners to be educated with them. The pupils entered the colleges at the age of eight or nine; they remained six years in the school, and during this time they were forbidden to leave it on any pretext whatever, even if they had relations in the neighbourhood. During the long vacation, which lasted from 15 September to 2 November, they had only one lesson a day and plenty of recreation.

St Germain drew up minute instructions for the conduct of the students. They were to dress themselves, keep their clothes in order, and to dispense with every kind of attendance. Up to the age of twelve their hair was to be cut short; afterwards a pigtail was to be worn, but powder was to be used only on Sundays and saint-days. The bed was to be simple, with only one rug, except in cases of delicate health. They were to receive a rude and vigorous education, calculated to form strong bodies, to have great liberty of movement and plenty of games, and not to be kept too long in school. They were not to waste their time in the writing of Latin verses, or oratorical themes; geography and history were to be learnt together. They were to read biographies of great men, and especially Plutarch's "Lives," and to feed their memories on the fine historic scenes of the French theatre. The study of mathematics was to be subordinate to that of the art of war, and that of drawing to fortification, castrametation, and military topography. Logic and ethics were to be taught without metaphysical superfluities. All corporal punishment was forbidden as injurious to the health, staining the soul, and depraving the character. These instructions form an interesting treatise on the principles of education.

When the boys had spent six years at the college and finished their education, they were to be placed as gentlemen cadets in his Majesty's army. For this purpose St Germain instituted an annual examination, to be held at Brienne in the beginning of September. Those who failed to pass remained at Brienne for a year longer, while those who distinguished themselves received exhibitions and medals. This scheme of St Germain was never carried into effect, but the colleges were inspected every year by government inspectors, each visit lasting ten days. Those of the King's scholars who seemed more fit to be priests or magistrates than soldiers were transferred to the college of La Flèche. The reports of these inspectors still exist, and are very interesting. We learn from them that the best of the military colleges was that of Pont-à-Mousson. Reynaud, the inspector, gives it unreserved praise. The classrooms, the refectories (where the canons dined at the same table with the boys), the playgrounds, the dormitories were excellent, and the pupils exhibited a good tone and perfect manners. Next to Pont-à-Mousson came Sorèze; Tiron, to which Napoleon was nearly sent, was out of the world, and its pupils were considered to be coarse and rough; the worst of all, perhaps, was Vendôme.

The college of Brienne, originally a monastery, was built at the foot of the hill on which the Château stands. It became a college in 1730, but had very few pupils, and in 1776 was made a royal military school. To meet these new duties the Minims spent not less than £6000. It held from a hundred to a hundred and fifty students. They slept in two corridors, each of which held seventy chambers, or cells, each of them six feet square, furnished with a strap bed, a water-jug, and basin. These cubicles were only used for sleeping, and were locked up at night. There was a bell communicating with the corridor, in which a servant slept. The classrooms were employed both for instruction and for private study. Meals were taken in a common dining-hall, large enough to contain a hundred and eighty persons, and the tables were served with sufficient generosity. The cadets changed their linen twice a week; they wore a blue coat with red facings and white metal buttons, with the arms of the college; their waistcoat was blue faced with white, their breeches blue or black according to circumstances; they wore an overcoat in winter. Their studies comprised Latin, which was their principal literary study, French poetry, but no Greek. The Latin authors studied were the Colloquies of Erasmus, Eutropius, Phædrus, Cornelius Nepos, Virgil, Cæsar, Sallust, Livy, Cicero, and Horace. It is interesting to know, in view of Napoleon's later career, that Vertot's *Histoire des Chevaliers de Malte* was regarded as a classical book, which had to be learned by heart or analyzed, and that the history of France, from the origin of the monarchy to the reign of Louis XVI, was studied, besides that of Greece and Rome. Geography was learnt, but no natural science; mathematics and German formed a regular part of the course. It seems natural for a people to learn the language of their last enemies. Drawing and dancing were learnt, and music up to 1783, when English was substituted for it. Napoleon wrote a bad hand, which Lucien attributed to the evil teaching of Brienne.

On the whole the school was in a bad state, and eventually fell into complete disorder. The Minims had probably undertaken a task beyond their powers. When Napoleon entered the establishment the Superior was Père Léluc, who was quite incompetent. After several warnings he was removed, and his place was taken by Père Louis Berton, who was rough and pompous, and was judged by Napoleon to be too hard. Schoolmasters of this type do not even succeed in securing discipline. His brother, Jean Baptiste Berton, was sub-principal, and is said to have been once a grenadier. The mathematical masters were Père Patrauld—whom Napoleon praised, and who was probably an excellent teacher—and Père Kehl, an Alsatian, who also taught German. Pichegru, the famous general, who is always spoken of as one of Napoleon's masters, had charge, in a subordinate capacity, of the elementary class, and gave Napoleon lessons at the end of 1779 or the beginning of 1780. He was very poor, and was nephew of a Sister of Charity who directed the infirmary. He desired to become a Minim, but Père Patrauld told him that he was reserved for something better. He entered the artillery in 1780, and commanded the army of the Rhine in 1793. Napoleon had a confused recollection of him as a tall man in a lay dress. French grammar was taught by Père Dupuy, and Napoleon conceived such a respect for his critical faculty that he submitted his first work, the *Lettres sur la Corse*, to his judgment before publication. His dancing master was Javilliers; and at the public speech day of 1781, Napoleon was one of the thirty-seven who gave a public exhibition of deportment, and one of seventeen who executed a country dance. In 1807 he asked the Countess Potocka how she thought he danced, "Sire," she said, "for a great man you dance perfectly." He danced, as consul, at the Malmaison, and Lucien said of him, "We are very fond of dancing, and Napoleon likes dancing and dances very well."

Such was the organization of the school of Brienne when Napoleon was studying there. The inspector, Reynaud, says of it that the boys are fairly well behaved, that their food is good, that the buildings are not bad; but that the teaching is weak in everything except mathematics, and that general culture is deficient. Reynaud says nothing about morals; but it is unfortunately true that Brienne was notorious for its immorality, and that it was deeply tainted with the vice which is too often found in large public boarding-schools. Indeed the "nymphs" of Brienne were proverbial. Napoleon was greatly horrified at this state of things, which offended at once his high principle, his purity, and his pride; and the stories which are told about his unsociability, if they have any truth, probably arise from his reluctance to mix with his companions upon their own terms. At the same time the boys were kept strictly to their religious exercises. Besides morning and evening prayer, they attended Mass every day and went to confession once a month. This *régime*, coupled with what has been mentioned above, rather tended to weaken Napoleon's religious beliefs. The boys were proud of the speed with which Mass could be said. Père Château got through his masses for the dead in four minutes and a half. Père Berton took ten minutes, and Père Avia eighteen or twenty minutes, and was voted a bore.

There is no doubt that Napoleon, while at Brienne, and especially at first, felt deeply the separation from his own beloved country, the room in which he was born, the garden in which he played, and the glorious sun of his native land. As a foreigner with a curious name he was naturally laughed at, and Napolionne, as he pronounced it, was turned into *La paille au nez*, "the straw on the nose"—not a very profound witticism. His teacher of geography persisted in describing Corsica as a dependency of Italy, an island conquered by France. Napoleon maintained his old enthusiasm for Paoli, and dreamed of some day recovering the independence of the island with his assistance. He lived a solitary existence, sullen and ill-tempered. Like the other students, he had a garden of his own, but he surrounded his with a palisade and planted it with trees. Here he spent his time dreaming and reading, driving off by force anyone who disturbed his solitude. He was naturally unpopular, as he admitted in after years; but he never complained to the monks, against whom he nourished a spirit of rebellion. Being flogged for this, he bore his punishment without a murmur; but once, having to do penance by dining on his knees at the door of the refectory, he was seized with such a violent attack of nerves that he became very ill, and his punishment had to be remitted.

Napoleon had no respect either for his teachers or his companions, and having no respect could have no affection. At last this state of things reached a crisis. The school was organized by the Principal in companies of cadets, and the command of one of these was given to Napoleon. But the other commanders held a court-martial in due form, and decided that Napoleon was unworthy to command his comrades because he disdained their affection. The sentence was read to him, and he was degraded from his rank; but he bore his humiliation with such gentleness that the hearts of the schoolboys were turned towards him. He became popular, lost his unsociability, and mingled with their games. During the severe winter of 1783 Napoleon built a square fort of snow with four bastions and a rampart three feet and a half long. The attack and defence were made with snowballs. In all these operations Napoleon distinguished himself by his activity and invention, constantly designing new manoeuvres. The fame of the fort spread beyond the school, and the townsmen of Brienne came to visit it.

During his stay at Brienne, Napoleon remained short of stature. His shoulders were broad, but his olive complexion gave him the appearance of ill-health. His eyes were bright and piercing, his forehead spacious and prominent, his lips delicately shaped, and his whole appearance denoted ardour and energy. He was very passionate, and his schoolfellows were afraid of him. His brother Lucien, who spent four months with him at Brienne, tells us that he received him without the slightest sign of emotion, that he was very serious, and not at all amiable in his manners. The effect of Brienne was to drive him back upon himself and to harden his personality. His whole soul was devoted to the profession of arms, and he began to be conscious that he was born to impose his will on others.

As to his studies, there is no evidence that he ever won a prize. He never learned Latin—indeed, French was to him a foreign language. He said once, what did it matter to him whether *amare* was of the first or of the second conjugation; what was the good of writing in a dead language? Napoleon did not encourage the study of Latin for soldiers; he formed a style of his own, which was not of a classical type. But Saint-Beuve has praised it, and has said that it shows *la griffe du lion* ("the lion's claw"). On the other hand, he was distinguished in mathematics, and advanced as far as conic sections. He was also remarkable for his knowledge of geography, but his favourite study was history. He was the most indefatigable reader in the school, and the books which he chose were generally historical. He devoured Plutarch with enthusiasm, and drew from his pages the desire and the resolution to be great. His favourite models were Leonidas and Dion, Curtius and Decius, Cato and Brutus. It is reported that one of his nicknames was "The Spartan," given to him on account of his admiration for that nation.

CHAPTER III

DEPARTURE FOR PARIS

On 21 June 1784, when he had been five years at Brienne, Napoleon was summoned to the parlour of the college to meet his father. Charles Bonaparte had come to France for various purposes: to petition the Controlleur-General about draining the salt marshes in Corsica; to consult the Paris doctors about his health, as he had suffered for some time from violent pains in the stomach; to conduct his daughter Marianna to the school of St Cyr; and to transfer his son Lucien from Autun to Brienne. This was the only visit which Napoleon had received during the whole of this long period from any of his family, and it was a gleam of sunshine. Charles remained two months at Paris, but was not able to pass by Brienne on his return to Corsica. Three days after his father's departure, Napoleon wrote the following letter to one of his uncles, perhaps his uncle Fesch:—

MY DEAR UNCLE,

"I write to inform you of the passage of my dear father by Brienne, on his way to Paris, to take Marianna to St Cyr, and to try to restore his health. He arrived here the 21st, with Luciano and the two young ladies, whom you have seen. He left my brother here, who is nine years of age, and three feet eleven inches and six lines tall. He is in the sixth class for Latin, and is intending to take all the different parts of the course. He shows much disposition and goodwill; we must hope that he will turn out well. He is in good health; is fat, lively, and mischievous, and for a beginning we are satisfied with him. He knows French very well, and has forgotten Italian entirely. He will write to you on the back of my letter; I shall tell him nothing, in order that you may see what he can do. I hope that now he will write to you more regularly than he did when he was at Autun. I am persuaded that Joseph, my brother, has not written to you. How would you expect him to do so? When he writes to my dear father, he writes only

27

two lines. In truth, he is no longer the same person. Nevertheless, he writes to me very often. He is in rhetoric, and would do very well if he worked; for the principal told my father that there was not in the college any one in the classes of physics, rhetoric, or philosophy who had as much talent as he had, or who wrote so good a version. As to the profession which he wishes to enter, the ecclesiastical was, as you know, the first he chose. He persisted in this resolution up to the present time, but now he wishes to serve the king. In this he is wrong, for several reasons—

(1) As my dear father remarks, he has not sufficient courage to face the dangers of an action. His feeble health does not permit him to bear the fatigues of a campaign, and my brother only looks at the military life from the point of view of a garrison. Yes, my dear brother would be a very good garrison officer, as he is well made, and has a ready wit, fitted for frivolous compliments, and with these qualities he will always come off well in society; but in a fight? That is what my dear father doubts.

(2) He has received an education for the ecclesiastical career; it is very late to give it up. Monseigneur, the Bishop of Autun, would have given him a fat benefice; and he was sure to be a bishop. What advantages for the family! Monseigneur d'Autun has done everything in his power to keep him to his resolution, promising him that he shall not repent it. No good; he persists. I praise him if it is the decided taste which he has for this profession—the finest of all pursuits, and the grand mover of human affairs—which, in forming him, has given him, as it has to me, a decided inclination for a military life.

(3) He wants to enter the army? Very well but in which branch? Will he enter the marine branch? He knows no mathematics, and it will take him two years to learn. Also, his health is incompatible with the sea. To be an engineer he will need four or five years to learn what he wants, and at the end of that time he will only be a probationer; besides, I think, the duty of working all day is not compatible with the levity of his character. The same reasoning holds good for the artillery, except that he has only to work eighteen months to be a probationer, and as much more to be officer. Oh! that is not yet to his taste. Let us see, then: he doubtless wishes to enter the infantry. Good! I understand him. He wishes to be all day without doing anything; he wishes to lounge about all day, and so much the more because he is only a tiny officer of infantry. That he should lead a good-for-nothing life three-fourths of his time is what neither my dear father, nor you, nor my mother, nor my dear uncle the archdeacon, will allow; and he has already shown some signs of levity and prodigality. Consequently, a last effort will be made to keep him to the Church, and

if this fails, my dear father will take him with him into Corsica, where he will have him under his eyes, and he will probably enter for the bar.

I conclude by begging you to continue to me your good graces. To render myself worthy of you will be the most important and the most anxious of my duties.

I am, with the most profound respect, your very humble and obedient servant and nephew,

NAPOLEONE DI BUONAPARTE.

P.S.—My dear uncle, tear up this letter; but one must hope that Joseph, with the talents which he has, and the sentiments with which his education ought to have inspired him, will take the good side, and will be the support of our family: represent to him a little all these advantages.

This is an extraordinary letter to have been written by a boy who was not yet fifteen years of age, and it does equal credit to his head and his heart. Joseph, however, was firm in his resolve, and determined to enter either the engineers or the artillery. His father yielded, and in July, 1784, solicited the minister, Ségur, to give him a commission. Ségur explained the difficulties of the examination, and Charles eventually withdrew him from Autun, and took him with him to Corsica. He had not seen his mother for five years.

Napoleon's answer to his father's letter, telling him that he was not able to visit him at Brienne, is worth transcribing, as it throws, like the last, so strong a light on his character. It runs thus:

MY DEAR FATHER,

"Your letter, as you may imagine, did not give me much pleasure; but reason, and the interests of your health and our family, which are very dear to me, made me praise your speedy return to Corsica, and have altogether consoled me.

Besides, being assured of the continuation of your goodness, and of your attachment, and of your efforts to get me out of this place, and to assist in everything that can give me pleasure, how could I be otherwise than contented? For the rest, I am eager to ask of you an account of the effects which the waters have had upon your health, and to assure you of my respectful attachment and of my eternal gratitude.

I am charmed that Joseph should have gone with you to Corsica, provided that he is here on November 1st, about a year from the present date. Joseph can come here, because Père Patrault, my mathematical master, whom you know, will not go away. In consequence, the principal has begged me to assure you that he will be received very well here, and that he can come in all security. Le Père Patrault is an excellent teacher of mathematics, and he has specially assured me that he will take charge of him with pleasure, and that if my brother will work, we can go together to the examination for the artillery. You need do nothing for me because I am already *élève*. Now you must do something for Joseph, but since you have a letter for him, all is said. So, my dear father, I hope that you will prefer to place him at Brienne, rather than at Metz, for several reasons. (1) Because it will be a consolation for Joseph, Lucien, and myself. (2) Because you will be obliged to write to the principal of Metz, which will produce delay, because you must wait for his answer. (3) It is not usual at Metz to learn what it is necessary that Joseph should know for the examination in six months, and in consequence, as my brother knows no mathematics, they will place him with the little children. These reasons, and many others, should induce you to send him here, and so much the more because he will be better off here. So I hope that before the end of October I shall embrace Joseph. For the rest, he need not leave before October 26th or 27th, to be here November next, 12th or 13th.

I beg you to send me Boswell (*History of Corsica*), with other histories or memoirs concerning this kingdom. You have nothing to fear; I will take care of them and will bring them back to Corsica with me when I come, if it is six years hence. Adieu, my dear father. The chevalier embraces you with all his heart. He works very well, and did very well at the public examination. The inspector will be here the 15th or 16th of this month at the latest. As soon as he is gone I will tell you what he has said to me. Present my respects to Minanna Saveria, Zia Gertruda, Zio Nicolino, Zia Touta, etc. Present my compliments to Minanna Francesca, Santo, Giovanna, Orazio; I beg you to take care of them. Give me news of them and tell me if they are well. I conclude by wishing you a health as good as my own.

Your very humble and very obedient

T.C. and son,

DE BUONAPARTE, l'arrière-cadet.

The chevalier mentioned in this letter is, of course, Lucien. It was the custom, both in schools and regiments, to call the younger of two noble brothers *chevalier*, brothers not noble were distinguished by the titles *ainè* and *cadet*. Lucien at this time was not a scholar of the establishment, as it was against rules to elect two scholars from the same family; he did not obtain a bourse or scholarship until Napoleon left.

Napoleon had at first intended to be a sailor. He hoped to be employed on the southern coasts of France, which would give him many opportunities of visiting his native island. The Corsicans were born sailors, and Napoleon was personally well fitted for the life. Keralio, the sub-inspector of the military schools, entered into these views. Napoleon attracted his attention in the years 1781 and 1782, and he hoped to be able to send him at an early age to the Military School at Paris, whence he could pass into the navy. But in 1783 Keralio was replaced as inspector by Reynaud de Monts, and when he visited Brienne in that year he formed a different judgment. Charles complained to the minister that the inspector had changed the career of his son, and begged that he might be removed from Brienne in order that Lucien might have his vacated scholarship. But in the meantime Napoleon had changed his mind. His mother dreaded the sea, and did not wish to expose him to the dangers of fire and water at the same time. Joseph excited his enthusiasm for the artillery, a corps in which merit had more influence than patronage or money, and we have seen from Napoleon's letter to his uncle how devoted he was himself to a military career. He expected to pass another year at Brienne, and that Joseph would join him there, so that the three brothers would be together. He would then, in 1785, present himself, with Joseph, for examination, to enter one of the artillery schools, and pass the examination for officer in the following year.

But, to his great surprise, the inspector, Reynaud, on his visit of 1784, chose Napoleon, with four others, to enter the Military School of Paris as gentlemen cadets. He probably owed this success to his mathematics, but the report of his performances has been lost, and that which is generally given by biographers is not authentic. Napoleon and his four companions left Brienne on 30 October 1784, and travelled to Paris, accompanied by one of the friars. It is possible that Napoleon owed his promotion to the fact that Reynaud had received permission to select cadets rather by promise than by performance, which is shown by his taking Laugier de Bellecour, who was a year-and-a-half younger than Napoleon, but who did not turn out well.

Brienne is always associated with the name of Napoleon; indeed, the full title of the town at the present day is Brienne-Napoleon. His statue stands in the market-place, and he left the town a million of francs in his will. It is satisfactory to know that the school was proud of him as a pupil. On 21 August 1800, a banquet was held in his honour at Paris, which was attended by the two Bertons, Patrauld, Bouquet, Avia, and Deshayes, together with some of the old pupils. Napoleon's bust was crowned with laurels, and the toasts were accompanied with the firing of cannon. The first toast was addressed to "General Bonaparte, our friend and comrade." He stayed at the Château of Brienne in 1805, on his way to Milan, but he found, to his distress, that the school buildings had been pulled down, and that only the convent remained which had been the lodging of the monks and the professors, as well as an avenue of limes, long dear to the old soldiers of the empire. He saw it again for the last time on 29 January 1814, when he had to take the château by force, and defend it against the Russians, an occasion on which Gourgaud saved his life. As he told those who were with him anecdotes of his school days, he said, "Could I then have believed that I should have to defend these places against the Russians!" On 1 February in the same year he lost, at Brienne, his first battle on French soil.

Napoleon never forgot a friend, and all those who were associated with him at Brienne had reason to be grateful to him. The porter of the school became the porter of Malmaison. His writing-master received a pension, although Napoleon said that in his case he had done little to deserve it. One of his teachers became librarian at Malmaison, where there were no books. To the priest who prepared him for his first communion, he gave a pension with an autograph letter. "I have not forgotten that it is to your virtuous example, and to your wise precepts, that I owe the high position that I have reached. Without religion no happiness, no success is possible. I recommend myself to your prayers." On passing through Dôle, in 1800, he sent for the same priest, when he was changing horses. The old man was deeply touched, and said to him, with tears, "Vale prosper et regna."

The parish priest of Brienne received an increase of income. He paid the debts of Père Patrault, and gave good positions to Berton and his family. We cannot follow the industry of M. Chuquet, who has traced the career of all those who were school-fellows of Napoleon at Brienne, so far as such information is attainable. The best known of them is Bourienne, whom he loaded with favours, but whom he was eventually obliged to dismiss for dishonesty in money matters. Bourienne was not at all an intimate friend of his at school, and the account which he has given in his memoirs of their school days is by no means trustworthy. Nansouty, one of the most brilliant cavalry officers of the empire, owed his advancement to his having been at Brienne. He became general of division, first chamberlain of the Empress, first equerry of the Emperor, commanded the cavalry of the Imperial Guard, and received vast sums in money and lands; but in 1814 he desired the fall of the empire, and deserted his benefactor in the midst of the battle of Laon. He was not the only one who repaid the kindness of the Emperor with gross ingratitude.

CHAPTER IV

THE ÉCOLE MILITAIRE DE PARIS

The École Militaire of Paris, founded by Louis XV, had been entirely reorganized by the Comte de St Germain in 1776. The old school had educated two hundred and fifty poor noblemen at great expense, and with luxury unbecoming the career of arms. The plan of the new minister was to educate six hundred students in the provinces, in such institutions as we have described, and to select the flower of these to be educated in Paris. The students, as in the provincial schools, were of two classes—*élèves*, paid for by the king, and *pensionnaires*, scholars and pensioners, or, as they would say at Eton, collegers and oppidans. The pensioners, like the *élèves*, must all be noble, and they cost their parents not less than a hundred a year, which by no means paid expenses. Scholars and pensioners were lodged, clothed, and fed in precisely the same manner, the idea being to establish a kind of honourable rivalry between them. But the scheme worked out differently. The pensioners seldom devoted themselves to serious study for the purpose of entering the engineers, the artillery, or the navy. They were sent to the school for the purpose of acquiring a general military education, and for having access to the magnificent riding-school, which had the reputation of being the best in Europe, after the king's own. The instruction of the two classes was the same, but one was industrious and the other idle.

When Napoleon entered the school the studies were arranged on the following principles: each lesson lasted two hours; each class contained from twenty to twenty-five students; each branch of study was taught by a single professor, and if he fell ill, his place was taken by a deputy. The whole body of cadets was arranged in two divisions, each containing three classes, formed, probably, according to the capacity of the pupils. The subjects of study were eight in number: mathematics, geography and history, French grammar, German grammar, fortification, drawing, fencing, and dancing. There were eight professors for each division, that is sixteen in all. The cadets worked eight hours a day—from seven to nine, from ten to twelve, from two to four, and from five to seven. Three days of the week were devoted to one set of four lessons, and the alternate days to the remaining set of four lessons. On Thursdays, Sundays, and festival-days the regular lessons were dropped, and the cadets passed four hours in their classrooms, two in the morning and two in the afternoon, writing letters and reading good books. This plan of studies had been drawn up in 1781, but in 1785 Latin grammar was introduced, and in 1784 a course of moral and political philosophy was added. In 1785 it became necessary to provide special teaching for those who were entering the scientific departments of the army. The young men were drilled every day, and on Thursdays and Sundays were exercised in firing. They were also taught most carefully the exercises of the drill-book, which they had to learn by heart. A few months before Napoleon entered the school the cadets had been organized as a regiment, with a commander-in-chief and other officers, who had authority over their comrades, and could inflict punishments out of school. The first commander-in-chief was Picot de Peccaduc, *élève* of artillery, but the students preferred to call him by the traditional name of sergeant-major, which Napoleon afterwards adopted.

The cadets changed their linen three times a week. The daily white shirt of the Etonian was not required, and they received new uniforms in April and October, which in Napoleon's time were blue with red facings. They naturally spent much of their time in the college court, as we should call it, surrounded by the classrooms. They hung up their hats and coats on pegs provided for the purpose, and played games, principally football and tennis. They also made use of a large open space called the promenade, in which a fort had been erected, called the Fort Timbrune. In bad weather they remained indoors, and played backgammon, chess, or draughts. The cadets slept in a large dormitory constructed of wood and warmed by earthenware stoves. Each cadet had a separate cubicle, simply furnished, with an iron bedstead, a chair, and a set of shelves. Sometimes, however, there was not sufficient room for all the students, and Napoleon occupied a chamber with his bosom friend, Desmazis. The parlour, in which visitors were received, was prettily furnished, and the classrooms were also made attractive. The École Militaire was one of the sights of Paris, and contemporaries of Napoleon could remember the visits of Joseph II, Gustavus III, and Prince Henry of Prussia.

The acting head of the school in Napoleon's time was a certain Valfort, whose real name was Silvestre, and who had risen by merit. He had the general direction of both the studies and the administration, and in this latter capacity had five officers under him; besides these there was a controller-general, a treasurer, or *bursar*, and an archivist. The school was governed by a Council of Administration, which met every month, presided over by the Minister of War; a Council of *Economie*, which met every week; and a Council of Police, which met three times a week. From which we may see that we have something to learn even today from the organization of the *ancien régime*. A college at Cambridge with one hundred and fifty undergraduates has ninety-six servants, and the École Militaire was not less fully provided. Among the professors were Legendre and Louis Monge, brother of the famous Gaspard Monge. Napoleon was taught geography by Tartas and Delesguille; both of whom he rewarded, especially the latter. French grammar was taught him by Domairon, the author of a rather remarkable book, *The General Principles of Literature*, which had a large sale and was translated into German. Napoleon never forgot him, and when he disappeared during the Revolution, took pains to seek him out, and in 1802 richly rewarded him. The cadets attended divine service twice a day, at six in the morning and at a quarter to nine in the evening; they went to confession every month. Founder's Day, in honour of Louis XV, was celebrated on 10 May. Napoleon received his first communion at Brienne, and he was confirmed at the École Militaire by the Archbishop of Paris, Juigne, whom, in 1808, he made a Count of the Empire. From the details we have given, it will be seen that the Royal Military School was one of the finest educational establishments in France, if not the first of all. It combined the prestige of antiquity and fashion with the reputation of having been remodelled to meet the requirements of a new and more exacting age. St Germain may not have contemplated, when he reformed the system of military education, that it would one day produce a Napoleon, but there can be no doubt that the career of the great soldier and administrator was profoundly influenced by the training which he had received, and that the debt of gratitude which he paid to his teachers was not undeserved.

The work in the school was very hard, and the discipline severe. The punishments consisted in arrest and imprisonment with or without bread and water. The cadets were not allowed to receive any money from their families, and no one, except the sergeant-major, was allowed to pass the gates. Napoleon might visit his sister, Marianna, at St Cyr only four times a year, and when he was leaving he received special permission to call on Bishop Marbœuf, accompanied by an officer. The standard of morality seems to have been higher than that of Brienne, as the boys were older and the tone was more manly. Also the discipline was sensibly exercised. Ségur wrote with regard to three students who were suspected of immoral practices, and whom it was proposed to send back to Pont-à-Mousson from whence they had come, that suspicion must not be taken for proof; that they should be watched carefully and drafted into the army as soon as possible; that to send them back to school would be to expose them to worse temptation, and would have a bad effect on the minds of the other boys. Also Laugier de Bellecour, of whom we have already spoken, began to go wrong, but the minister refused to approve the recommendation of the Council to send him back to Brienne. A serious attempt was made to give the cadets a good education and to fit them to be men of the world, to teach them to write and converse correctly, and to have good manners. We must remember that at this time French education and erudition gave the law to Europe in these respects. The Revolution, like the Reformation, set the clock of culture back for many hours. Napoleon afterwards complained that the school was too luxurious, but the same thing may be said of many of our English colleges. It was estimated that each cadet cost the Royal Treasury £170, and on this account, when economies were being made in 1787, the school was suppressed. When it became the duty of Napoleon to found military colleges of his own, he borrowed many things from the École Militaire, and declared that the old monarchy had acted very wisely and had received the sanction of experience. But he made his cadets groom their own horses and sweep their own rooms. No servants were allowed, the students cooked their own food and cut their own wood, they fed on garrison bread, and were allowed only half a bottle of wine a day.

The sojourn of Napoleon at the École Militaire was saddened by the death of his father, which took place on 24 February 1785. Often on his couch of agony he asked for Napoleon. "Where is Napoleon," he cried; "where is my son Napoleon, whose sword will make kings tremble, who will change the face of the world? He will protect me from my enemies, he will save my life!" The utterance of these strange prophetic words is attested by both Fesch and Joseph, who were both of them present when they were spoken. He died, and was buried at Montpellier, but his body was afterwards transferred to the crypt of the church of St Leu. Napoleon felt his father's death severely. We have the letters which he wrote to his uncle, the archdeacon, and to his mother on the subject, but they have evidently been corrected by the masters of the school, and are scarcely worth reproducing. In the first he asks the Archdeacon Lucien to assume the position of the head of the family.

Napoleon had now to prepare himself for the examination which would secure his admission into the artillery. For this purpose the following arrangements had been made in the year 1779. A person wishing to become an officer of artillery, had first to become an aspirant. This was effected by his receiving what we should call a nomination from the Minister of War to be admitted to the examination, the conditions of obtaining which we need not specify. The examination was held at Metz. If the aspirant failed to pass, he might present himself a second time; if he passed he entered some school of artillery as an *élève*, and the following year could go in for his examination as officer. If he succeeded he received the rank of second lieutenant, if he failed he might try a second time, but he was rigorously excluded from a third competition. These examinations were almost entirely confined to a single book, the *Cours de Mathematiques*, written by Bezout. To become an *élève* an aspirant must know the first volume of Bezout, which contained arithmetic, geometry, and trigonometry. But to become an officer it was necessary to be well acquainted with the other three volumes of Bezout: the second, which treated of algebra and of the application of algebra to geometry; the third, which dealt with mechanics, hydrostatics, and the differential and integral calculus; and the fourth, which was concerned with still higher subjects. At the same time, if an aspirant was thoroughly well acquainted with all four volumes of Bezout, he might become an officer without having been an *élève*.

The artillery school of Metz, which had excellent teachers and an admirable tradition, generally obtained the first place in these competitions. Bezout and Laplace, who were the examiners of the school, had a great influence over its teaching. Bezout said that Metz was a precious resource for the artillery, and Laplace was desirous to collect as many students as possible in that town. But in 1785 the Military School of Paris, which had improved in 1784, had an unprecedented success. Eighteen candidates were presented for the examination, including Laugier de Bellecour, who was not yet fifteen, but he was eventually withdrawn. Napoleon was examined by the great Laplace in the second week of September, in a room of the Military School specially provided for that purpose, and the result was known about a fortnight afterwards. Out of the whole number of candidates, fifty-eight were admitted as officers—four of whom came from the Paris school. Of these Bonaparte was third, being beaten by Phélipeaux, who had beaten him before, and by Picot de Peccaduc, who was a year older. The fourth name was that of Desmazis, and the order in the whole list was Picot de Peccaduc 39, Phélipeaux 41, Bonaparte 42, and Desmazis 56. Thus Napoleon attained the honour of passing over the rank of *élève* and being made officer at once, having been only one year at the school. He owed his success to his diligent study of Bezout, and we find the following lines scribbled by him on the flyleaf of the fourth volume:—

Grand Bezout, áchève ton cours.
Mais avant, permets-moi de dire
Qu'aus aspirants tu donnes secours.
Celà est parfaitement vrai.
Mais je ne cesserai pas de rire
Lorsque je ı'aurai achevè
Pour le plus tard au mois de mai,
Je ferai alors le conseiller.

Which may be interpreted—

Great Bezout, thy course complete,
First allow me to repeat
Many a candidate you aid.
This by none can be gainsaid.
But I see the time approach
When I've read your last big tome,
When the month of May has come,
Then I'll laugh and turn a coach.

He means by this that he will have finished his own work four months before the examination, and will then be able to take it easy and to instruct his companions.

Napoleon did not specially distinguish himself at the École Militaire. He was never sergeant-major, nor commander of a division, nor head of a mess; but he won his promotion, after ten months' work, above some of those who had beaten him at Brienne. He was able to boast, in 1788, that he had profited by the benefits of the king, and had, by assiduous labour, succeeded in entering the artillery at the first examination.

Laplace was an excellent and sympathetic examiner, and Napoleon never forgot him. When the great mathematician dedicated to him his famous work, *La Mecanique Celeste*, Napoleon replied that its perusal gave him an additional reason for regretting that the force of circumstances had driven him into a career which was so far removed from scientific study. On receiving the *Traité de Probabilités* during his Russian campaign, the Emperor wrote to the author from Vitebsk that it was one of those works which bring to perfection mathematics—the first of sciences—and contribute to the glory of the nation. Napoleon, as First Consul, made him Minister of the Interior, for which, as might be expected from a mathematician, he was eminently unfit. He afterwards made him Senator,

Chancellor of the Senate, Grand Officer of the Legion of Honour, and Count of the Empire. A curious interview is reported to have taken place between them in 1813, after the defeat of Leipzig. The Emperor said to him, "You have changed, and grown very thin." "Sire," replied Laplace, "I have lost my daughter." Napoleon replied, "You, a geometrician, submit this event to your calculus, and you will find that it equals zero." This speech does not belong to the life or character of the young Napoleon.

It is interesting to inquire into the career of Napoleon's most brilliant companions who entered the artillery at the same time as himself. Picot de Peccaduc was the pet boy of the school; he performed the duties of sergeant-major, or captain, with distinguished success, and received a valuable present from the Council in recognition of his services. He emigrated, entered the Austrian army, and was twice taken prisoner by his former schoolfellow. In 1811 he took the name of Herzogenberg, as he had renounced for ever the citizenship of France. He was present at the battles of Dresden and Culm. At the close of his life he became head of an Austrian academy which resembled the École Militaire, and died at the age of sixty-seven. Phélipeaux and Napoleon detested each other at school, and Picot, who sat between them to prevent their quarrels, had to give up the task because he received kicks from both sides. Phélipeaux emigrated early, and joined the army of Condé, but returned to France and effected the escape of Sidney Smith from the Temple, accompanying him to England. He then went with Sidney Smith to Syria, and was his most powerful assistant in the defence of St Jean d'Acre against Napoleon, which was a turning-point in Napoleon's career. As Las Cases remarked at St Helena, it is strange that the two who commanded on that occasion should have belonged to the same nation, be of the same age, be members of the same branch of the service, and have sat next to each other in the same school. Luckily for Napoleon, Phélipeaux died during the siege. The relations between Alexandre Desmazis and Napoleon were almost of a romantic kind. When he entered the military school Napoleon was attached to him for preliminary infantry instruction, according to a custom which still prevails at Winchester, and used to exist at King's College, Cambridge, and perhaps at other places. As I have before mentioned, they occupied the same room. Desmazis was just a year older than his bosom friend. He had refined and charming manners, but was somewhat passionate in disposition, and was susceptible to the charms of the other sex. Napoleon chided him on this head, and recommended the example of his own cold tranquillity. At the same time, when he passed his examination for lieutenant, the inspector spoke of him as very industrious, very zealous, of good character and conduct, and setting the best example. Desmazis was the companion of Napoleon both at Valence and Auxonne, but in 1792 he emigrated, and served for three years in the English army, and then in the army of Portugal. Napoleon never forgot him. Returning to France in 1802, he was made administrator of the Crown buildings, and, resigning in 1814, he was again restored in the following year. He was living in 1833, and it is a pity that he never wrote his memoirs. The Emperor was as generous to his friend's family as to himself. Those who wish to study the career of the rest of Napoleon's comrades must read them in the laborious and fascinating pages of M. Chuquet. The great majority of them joined the emigration; their heart, as Napoleon expresses himself, was not blue but white, but those whom he was able to employ he never neglected.

It would be interesting to know what impression Napoleon made at this time upon his teachers, and whether they had any presentiment of his destined eminence. As might be expected, when he became famous, they were ready to exclaim that they had not only taught the boy, but had foreseen, and perhaps stimulated, his future glory. English Public Schools often claim as their most distinguished triumphs those whom as boys they rejected and despised. We know, however, that Baur, the teacher of German, thought him an idiot. One day in September, 1785, Baur noticed that Napoleon was not present in class, and was told that he was in for the artillery examination. "Does he know anything?" asked Baur. "Why, he is one of the best mathematicians in the school," was the reply. "Ah," said Baur, "I have always thought that only idiots were fit to study mathematics." Napoleon, it is true, learnt French, but he had little faculty for foreign tongues, as we learn from his clumsy attempts at a later period to acquire English.

We know, however, that Napoleon, at the military school, as at Brienne, showed the signs of a deep and serious character. He was very industrious and very thoughtful. Once, when his chum Desmazis was absent at the infirmary, he shut himself up in his rooms for three days, with doors and shutters closed, reading by lamplight. He also had many a fight with the scions of the high nobility who despised the *elévès*, the oppidans who bullied the collegers. He had lost the sombre taciturnity which distinguished him at Brienne, and had become more companionable. He lived in a military atmosphere, and not amongst monks and schoolboys. His friendship with Desmazis gave a touch of romance to his life, and there was less of the gross immorality which at Brienne estranged him from his companions. At the same time, his standard of conduct was very high and his attitude uncompromising. He said to Laugier de Bellecour, "You are forming connections of which I do not approve; I have succeeded in keeping your morals pure, and your new friends will destroy you. Choose between them and me; there is no middle course; be a man, and decide." Laugier said that Napoleon was mistaken, and that he was unchanged in friendship. "Make the choice," replied Napoleon, "and take my words for a first warning." Laugier did not improve, and some time later he gave him a second caution; but on a third occasion Napoleon said, "You have despised my warnings, you have renounced my friendship, never speak to me again."

Still Napoleon remained a thorough Corsican. He was never tired of telling his companions that he would willingly have fought by the side of Paoli. He began a poem on the liberty of Corsica, which he recited to Laugier with a drawn sword in his hand. A caricature of Napoleon drawn at this time by one of his comrades is extant, in which he is represented with a stick held by both hands, and a stern and determined look, stalking forth to join Paoli, with the legend underneath, "Bonaparte, run, fly to the assistance of Paoli, to rescue him from the hands of his enemies." As at Brienne, he denounced the injustice, the ungenerosity, of a war waged by a great people against a tiny nation. The opinions of Napoleon came to the ears of the authorities. Valfort sent for him, and said, "Sir, you are a scholar of the King; you must learn to remember it, and to moderate your love for Corsica, which, after all, forms part of France." This speech did not produce the desired effect, and one day a priest at the confessional rebuked him on the same subject. Napoleon ran back into the church, and cried, loud enough for his companions to hear him, "I do not come here to talk about Corsica, and a priest has no mission to lecture me on that subject." These anecdotes, and many others which are less well authenticated, evince, at any rate, the strength and independence of his character.

CHAPTER V

VALENCE AND AUXONNE

On leaving the École Militaire, Napoleon and Desmazis were attached to the regiment of La Fère, which was then quartered at Valence. Desmazis wished to join that regiment because his elder brother was captain in it, and Napoleon because Valence was on the road to Corsica, and the artillery garrison of that island was always taken from the regiment of La Fère. Napoleon left the École Militaire on 28 October 1785. He spent that day and the next in making preparations for his journey, and in paying visits, especially to Marbœuf, the Bishop of Autun, to whom he owed so much. All this time he was accompanied by a non-commissioned officer, who did not lose sight of him until he got into the diligence which was to convey him to his garrison. He left Paris on 30 October, together with Desmazis and Delmas, who was going to Valence as an *élève*. He took with him twelve shirts, twelve collars, twelve pairs of socks, twelve handkerchiefs, two nightcaps, four pairs of stockings, a pair of shoe-buckles, a pair of garter-buckles, one sword, and a silver collar-stud; also about £6 10s for the journey. To his disappointment, he still wore the uniform of the school.

The two young officers travelled by the Lyons diligence, one of the best equipped in the kingdom. They dined the first day at Fontainebleau, afterwards so fatally woven with the fate of one of them, and slept at Sens, and then, passing by Autun, reached Chalons-sur-Saône. Here they took the water-diligence, and went down the Saône to Lyons. From Lyons they travelled in a single day by post boat to Valence, a difficult and sometimes dangerous journey.

It was only since 1783 that a school of artillery had been definitely established at Valence. The garrison now consisted of seven regiments of artillery, nine companies of workmen, and six of miners. The artillery regiments were composed of gunners, bombardiers, and sappers. Each

43

regiment of artillery was divided into two battalions, and contained twenty companies; that is, fourteen companies of gunners, four of bombardiers, and two of sappers. Each battalion formed two brigades, of which the first contained four companies of gunners; the second, three companies of gunners, and one of sappers. The four companies of bombardiers constituted a fifth brigade. Each brigade was commanded by a brigadier with the rank of major. Each company, consisting of seventy-one men, was commanded by a captain and three lieutenants, the third lieutenant being drawn from the ranks.

The regiment of La Fère was one of the best in the French army; it was animated by the spirit of work and early rising, and its drill was as perfect as that of an infantry regiment. Three days a week were given to the study of theory and three to artillery practice. It was also a smart corps, and was popular in the towns in which it was quartered. The tone of the officers was excellent.

It was in this regiment that Napolionne de Buonaparte, as he is called in official documents, began to serve as second lieutenant; his colonel being M. de Lance, his lieutenant the Vicomte d'Urtubie, and his major an old man, M. de Labarrière, who had distinguished himself in the seven years' war. He now put on the artillery uniform, which he always declared to be the most beautiful in the world; blue, with red facings, marked with the number 64, the artillery being reckoned as the 64th regiment of infantry. He began to drill, like all the cadets of that period, first as a private, then as a corporal, and then as a sergeant; and did not assume his duties as an officer till January, 1786, when the commander of the school considered him to be sufficiently instructed. His work was hard and continuous: it comprised mounting guard, looking after his bombardiers—to which company he was attached—attending the school of theory, lectures on mathematics, fortification, physics, and chemistry, drawing lessons, and professional discussions; and going every morning after his labours to a pastrycook's shop, eating two patties—which cost him a penny—and drinking a glass of water. His income was about £50 a year, and was made up of £36 pay, £5 for lodgings, £8 from the École Militaire, and a little private assistance from his uncle Lucien. He lodged on the first floor of a house situated at the corner of the Grand Rue and the rue du Croissant, belonging to a Mlle Bou, and he dined at the Three Pigeons, in the rue Pérollerie. He was very comfortable with M. Bou and his daughter, who was an old maid of fifty, and mended his linen. When he left for Auxonne, M. Bou said to him, "We shall never see each other again, and you will forget us." Napoleon placed his hand on his heart, and replied, "You are

lodged here, and memories once established here never change garrison."
When he returned from Egypt he met Mlle Bou at the gate of Valence, and
presented her with an Indian shawl and a silver compass. As has already
been said, the tone of the regiment was excellent, and the officers lived
together like a happy family. Napoleon has borne testimony to this, and
tells us that his superior officers were the most brave and the most worthy
people in the world, pure as gold, but too old in consequence of the long
peace. The younger officers laughed at them because it was the tone of the
age; but they admired them, and always did them justice.

Although Napoleon now took lessons in dancing and deportment,
which he had neglected at the École Militaire, and M. Dautel, his
instructor, boasted that he had directed his first steps in the world, yet
he never acquired the distinguished manners of the old *régime*, which he
afterwards admired in his brother Louis, but remained shy, awkward, and
ill at ease. At the same time he was popular, and received great kindness
from many people. One of his principal friends was the mitred abbot of
St Ruf, who had retired on a pension after the suppression of his order,
and to whom the Bishop of Autun had given an introduction. The Hotel
St Ruf was the centre of the best society of the town, who were attracted
by the excellence of the abbot's dinners. Three ladies also paid the young
officer particular attention, Mme Lauberie de Saint-Germain, Mme de
Laurencin and Mme Grégoire de Colombier. Of these, Mme de Colombier
had the greatest influence upon him. She invited him to her country house
at Basseaux, and gave him excellent advice. She predicted a great career
for him, and warned him not to emigrate, saying that it was easy to go out,
but not so easy to return. She had a daughter Caroline, of the same age as
himself, whom Napoleon loved as a friend. He mentions some delicious
moments which he passed with her, eating cherries. It is possible that he
gave his sister Maria Nunziata the name of Caroline in her honour. He
corresponded with her when Emperor, and did everything he could for her
relations and friends. She eventually became lady-in-waiting to Madame
Mère. He was, perhaps, still more touched by the charms of Mlle de
Lauberie de Saint-Germain, who was afterwards made lady-in-waiting
to Josephine. He also made many excursions in the neighbourhood, one
of them into Dauphiné, where he ascended the Roche-Colombe, in June,
1786, and another of them to Tournon, where lived a countryman of his,
named Pontornini, who drew his first portrait.

Napoleon had the right to six months' leave after a year's service, and
he looked forward passionately to spending this time in Corsica. He
writes in a curious paper, dated 3 May 1786, in which he contrasts the

desire with which he is longing to visit Corsica with the disappointment which he is sure to experience upon his arrival at seeing his beloved island enslaved by the French, so that he is tempted to contemplate suicide. "I have been absent from my country for six or seven years. What pleasure it will give me in a few months to see once more my compatriots and my relations! With the tender emotions which the recollections of my childhood evoke, may I not conclude that my happiness will be complete?" But before he could carry out this plan, he was sent with his company to Lyons to put down a strike among the workmen for higher wages. Three artisans were hanged, and the sedition was rapidly quelled. Napoleon spent three weeks at Lyons, and then returned to Valence, which he left for Corsica on 1 September 1786. His leave did not legally commence till 1 October, but officers living as far off as Corsica were allowed a month's grace. At Aix, he visited his uncle Fesch, who had not yet completed his theological studies, and his brother Lucien, who had left Brienne and entered the Seminary of Aix to be trained as a priest. He reached Ajaccio on 15 September 1786; he had been absent seven years and nine months, and was now seventeen years and one month old. There was probably no man living who contained so much genius and energy, so much vivacity and charm, and, one may add, such high aims and such determination to carry them out, in so small and so comely a person.

Joseph writes in his memoirs: "My brother Napoleon at last obtained leave. He arrived among us, and it was a great happiness for our mother and for myself. We had not seen each other for several years, but we corresponded habitually by letter. The aspect of the country pleased him. His habits were those of an industrious and studious young man, but he was very different from what he is represented to be by authors of memoirs, who repeat the same mistake when it has been once uttered. He was at that time a passionate admirer of Rousseau, the inhabitant of an ideal world, a lover of the great works of Corneille, of Racine, of Voltaire, which we declaimed together every day. He had collected a number of books, which occupied a trunk larger than that which contained his clothes—the works of Plutarch, of Plato, of Cicero, of Cornelius Nepos, of Livy, and of Tacitus, all translated into French, besides the writings of Montaigne, of Montesquieu, and of Raynal. I do not deny that he had also with him the poems of Ossian, but I deny that he preferred them to Homer."

He saw once more, with indescribable pleasure, his mother, his brother Joseph, and his great-uncle Lucien. Joseph said, many years afterwards, "Ah! the glorious Emperor will never indemnify me for Napoleon, whom I loved so well, and whom I should like to meet again as I knew him in

1786, if there is indeed a meeting in the Elysian Fields." He saw once more his two grandmothers, Minanna Severia and Minanna Francesca, his uncle Paravicini, and his aunt Gertrude, his foster-mother, and his devoted nurse. He stood godfather to the granddaughter of Camilla Ilari, the future Madame Poli. He traversed with emotion the scene of his first games; being passionately fond of natural beauty, he wonders that anyone can be insensible to the "electricity of nature." He spent hours in the garden of Milelli, either in the rocky grotto, or in the dense olive woods, or under a large oak tree, drawing, reading, and dreaming. In the evening he wandered amongst the sheep in the meadows, or from the sea-shore watched the sun "precipitate himself into the bosom of the infinite," possessed by a melancholy which he could not master. The love of Corsica came back to him with a tenfold ardour, the very smell of the earth intoxicated him with pleasure. He was received everywhere with open arms, in the solitude of the mountains and in the peasant's hut.

At the same time his chief care was directed to the interests of his family, which had lost its two powerful protectors, Boucheporn and Marbœuf, the one dead, the other removed to the Pyrenees. From the moment Napoleon arrived he was the soul of the house, of which during his absence the Archdeacon Lucien had been the acting head. He had many discussions with his uncle on the policy of keeping goats, which destroyed the trees and made the higher agriculture impossible. Fesch was of the same opinion, but Lucien, who was a large goat proprietor, was shocked. "These are your philosophical ideas! Drive the goats out of Corsica!" The archdeacon was now sixty-eight years old, and was a martyr to gout, being confined to his bed. Joseph, in obedience to his father's last wishes, had given up his project of a military career, and had devoted himself entirely to the care of his family. He now left Corsica, and by the advice of his uncle went to the University of Pisa, where, like his father, he took his degree, *in utroque jure*, on 24 April 1788. The absence of Joseph increased the responsibilities of his younger brother, and one of the most important matters which he had to arrange concerned a nursery of mulberry trees. In 1782 Charles Bonaparte had received from the government leave to make a nursery of mulberry trees, for which he was to be paid 8500 livres in advance, and one sol per tree for grafting, with the obligation of setting out the trees five years later in 1787. He had received 5800 livres, but the contract was annulled in May, 1786. The Bonapartes had made their plantation, but the Minister refused to sanction any further expense. Napoleon came to the conclusion that his family had been ill-treated, and demanded an indemnity to the extent of 1550 livres, expended before the contract was rescinded, and 1500 livres for the grafting, making a total of 3050 livres. These 3050 livres added to the 5800 livres already received, would make a sum of 8850 livres, which his mother would owe to the government. But this debt could be easily repaid, as the mulberry trees would be worth at least 9000 livres.

Napoleon's leave, which ought to have come to an end at the end of March, was extended to 1 December 1787 on the faith of a medical certificate sent to Colonel de Lance, stating that he was suffering from an attack of fever. There is no reason to doubt the truth of this, as Napoleon mentions it in a letter addressed to Doctor Tissot, written about his uncle's illness. As, however, it was necessary that he should visit Paris on his family affairs, he left Corsica on 12 September, having stayed there just a year. He now became acquainted with Paris for the first time, as when at the École Militaire he had been kept strictly within the four walls. He lodged at the Hotel de Cherbourg, Rue Four St Honoré. He visited the theatres, especially the Italian Opera, and walked in the gardens and passages of the Palais Royal. Among the Libri MSS. there is a curious paper, dated 22 November 1787, which narrates a conversation which he is supposed to have held with a woman of the town in one of the alleys of the Palais Royal. The document is interesting, and M. Masson has printed a facsimile of it. It is probably a mere exercise in composition, or it may have had some slight foundation in fact. But it certainly does not imply, as Napoleon's French biographers, with characteristic *naïveté*, all assume, that the young officer deviated on this occasion from the stern principles of virtuous conduct which he both taught and practised at this period. To believe that he did so is to misunderstand his nature, and if he had done so he would certainly have said nothing about it. He probably visited his sister, Marianna, at St Cyr, but his chief attention was given to his mother's claim, which he pressed with all the force of his intellect before the Controller-General, but without success. In the midst of these occupations his period of leave would naturally have come to an end, but on 7 September, before leaving Corsica, he had asked for a prolongation on the ground that he desired to be present at the meeting of the Corsican Estates. Apparently in the Regiment de La Fère leave was granted very easily, and as he did not ask for his pay, the desired prolongation was accorded to him from 1 December 1787 to 1 June 1788.

Napoleon returned to Ajaccio on 1 January 1788, and found his mother in great poverty. She had four young children to support, Louis aged ten, Pauline eight, Caroline six, and Jerome four. She had also to pay the fees of Lucien at Aix and of Joseph at the University of Pisa. She could not keep a servant or pay her debts. Napoleon did his best to help his mother. He laboured to obtain for his brother Louis a scholarship in a military school, and to urge on the planting of the mulberry trees and the draining of the salt marshes, which were of such vital consequence to the family finances, but without result. We need not pursue these matters further, as they dragged on for many a year, even till after his position was assured.

On 1 June 1788, Napoleon again left Ajaccio, after having seen his brother Joseph on his return from Pisa with the title of Doctor. He had been absent from his regiment for twenty-one months. But these indulgences were common under the *ancien régime*. The colonel was only required to be present with his regiment for five months in the year, the lieutenant-colonel and the major divided the year between them, and the other officers took their *semestre*, which in 1788 was declared officially to last seven months and a half. It is unfair to censure Napoleon, as some biographers have done, for irregularities which were common to the whole of the army, or to suppose that in devoting himself to the service of his family instead of to the exercise of a profession which he loved he was not obeying the voice of duty rather than that of pleasure.

The regiment of La Fère, which had made many marches during the absence of Napoleon, was now at Auxonne, where it had arrived in December, 1787, when the danger of a war between France and England was at an end. Napoleon lodged in the Pavilion de la Ville, at the side of the barracks. His room had a single window, and was simply furnished with a bed, a table, and an armchair; there were also six chairs seated with straw and one with wood. The climate did not suit him, as it was both damp and cold, and it took him six months to acclimatize himself after the dry and bracing air of Corsica. He worked very hard—too hard, indeed, for his health. He wrote in July 1789, "I have nothing to do here except work; I only put on my uniform once a week. I sleep very little since my illness; I go to bed at ten and get up at four, and have only one meal a day." That Napoleon was engaged in hard and continuous labour during the fifteen months which he spent at Auxonne we have abundant proof. The Libri MSS contain twenty-seven papers written by the young lieutenant at this time, which are only a part of those which he actually composed. They may be divided into three categories: those concerned with the study of his profession as an artillery officer; those concerned with the general history of mankind—especially their government,—and including geography; and those concerned with Corsica. We thus see that Napoleon had determined, with his iron will, to give himself a complete education, which would not only fit him to be distinguished in his profession, but to occupy any civil profession which the course of life might place in his way. He realized what in the present day is apt to be forgotten—that a soldier has sometimes to perform functions which more properly belong to the statesman, and that unless he is equal to the task of concluding peace as well as making war, and of governing the territories which his sword has subdued, the interests of his country may materially suffer. Some of these papers belong especially to this period. The first of these, written probably in September 1788, is a project for organizing the "Calotte" of the regiment—that is, an association formed among the officers under the rank of captain, for the purpose of maintaining good order and discipline, and a high standard of conduct among themselves, as well as of defending themselves against arbitrary action on the part of their chiefs. The project is of considerable length, and is conceived in too solemn a style to have been acceptable to the frivolous young gentlemen for whose benefit it was composed. Indeed, the fair copy presented by him was probably thrown into the fire. But the work is interesting as the first of those constitutions of which Napoleon was destined in after years to draft so many, and, like them, it bears unmistakable signs of the "lion's claw." There is also a certain grim humour in the document which ought not to escape notice. The papers on artillery practice have an interest for the student of military history, and are remarkable productions for a young man of less than twenty years of age. Of the papers on Corsica one set has been lost, the letters on Corsica addressed to M. Necker.

Although Napoleon was at this time ill and out of spirits, we must not suppose that he led a morose or solitary life. Besides his inseparable companion Desmazis, he had many warm friends, whose careers offer abundant proof of their mutual attachment. One of these, after being treated most generously by the Emperor, was in 1815 nominated Prefect of the "Eure et Loir," when it was found that he had already joined the Bourbons. The most remarkable of the captains who belonged at this time to the regiment of La Fère was Gassendi. He was a distinguished geometer and also a man of letters; he was also a great admirer of Corsica and the Corsicans. He was one of the first to recognize the genius of Napoleon and to hail him as the new Cæsar, chosen by victory to impose upon France a yoke radiant with glory. The Emperor amply repaid his devotion.

There is no reason for supposing that Napoleon was unsociable during his stay at Valence or at Auxonne, or that he was anything but a good fellow. The cameraderie of the military profession always distinguished him through life, and remained with him at St Helena up to the day of his death. It is most prominent in the pages of Marbot, and it gave him great power over his soldiers in the Italian campaigns. He was a constant guest at the regimental dinners, cooked by Faure, at the Écu de France at Valence, and many stories are told of him which enforce the same conclusion. The fact that he was chosen by his comrades to draft a constitution for "La Calotte," is a proof that he possessed their confidence.

At Auxonne Napoleon completed his instruction as officer of artillery; he worked hard and came out one of the very best. The notes which he took of the lectures of his instructor Lombard are still preserved; they deal with the pressure of powder, its ignition, the action of the air on projectiles, the utility of large and small charges and of rifled cannon. The young officer also greatly improved his skill as a draughtsman, although the drawings of Napoleon must always have been botches. On 3 August 1788, he was appointed a member of a commission to study the firing of certain cannon, and he alone of the second lieutenants was a member of it. His duty was to place the pieces in position and to draw up the report. On 29 August he wrote to Fesch, "You must know, my dear uncle, that the general here has treated me with great consideration, and has charged me to construct at the shooting-range several works which require severe calculations; and I have been occupied morning and evening for ten days, the head of two hundred men. This unheard-of mark of favour has irritated the captains a little against me, who say that it is a slur upon them to charge a lieutenant with so important a duty, and that as there are more than thirty who could do the work, one of them ought to have been employed. My comrades also show a little jealousy, but all that will pass away." The report drawn up by Bonaparte still exists, and may be interesting to experts. Further, in March 1789, he wrote a paper in which he set forth his personal views as to the best manner of placing cannon for the purpose of firing bombs.

It was at Auxonne that Napoleon came into contact with the family of Du Teil, which had some influence over his early career. The school of artillery at Auxonne was commanded by the maréchal de camp, Baron Jean-Pierre Du Teil, an excellent officer, if somewhat severe. He was proud of his artillery school, which indeed had the reputation of being the best in France, and was visited by distinguished men when they came to the country. Prince Henry of Prussia and Gustavus III of Sweden inspected the school in 1784, and the two Princes of Wurtemburg in 1788. Du Teil soon remarked the talents of Napoleon, and the Emperor showed his gratitude by leaving in his will a hundred thousand francs to the sons or grandsons of his former chief, "in return for the care which this brave general had bestowed upon him."

Whilst at Auxonne he was put under arrest, but the reason is not known. In 1806 he met a Captain Floret, and said to him, "Do you remember that at Auxonne Sergeant Floret was put in prison for a week, and Lieutenant Bonaparte for twenty-four hours?" "Yes, sire," replied Floret, "you were always more fortunate than I was." He was shut up in a room with an old chair, an old bed, and an old cupboard, and on the top of the cupboard was an old worm-eaten book, a copy of the *Digest*. Napoleon, having no paper or ink, devoured the one book at his disposal, and the knowledge of it thus gained proved useful to him at a later period, when he was drawing up the *Code Napoléon*. At the beginning of April 1789, he was sent with his bombardiers to put down some grain riots at Seurre, one of those disturbances which were precursors of the coming revolution. The riots had ceased before he arrived, but he stayed two months in the little town, lodging in the rue Dulac, which afterwards bore the name of the rue Bonaparte, and where the rooms which he occupied were long shown. He returned to Auxonne on 29 May.

In the summer of 1789 Napoleon met with a serious accident, which might have cost him his life. As he was bathing in the Saône he was seized with cramp and was nearly drowned. But, being carried down by the stream to a shallow part of the river, he managed to recover himself, and, after being very sick, he was conveyed by his friends to his lodgings.

In the summer of 1789 the contagion of the Revolution reached Auxonne. On 19 July, five days after the destruction of the Bastille, the populace broke into revolt, burned the register of taxes, and destroyed the offices. The regiment of La Fère took the part of the rioters, and a month later broke out into open mutiny. They marched to the colonel's house, demanded a sum of money, called the "masse noire," from the military chest, got drunk with it, and compelled the officers to drink with them and to dance the farandole. In consequence of this the regiment was broken up, and quartered in different places along the banks of the Saône. Undoubtedly, at this time, if Napoleon had been forced to act, he would not have hesitated to turn his guns against the people. At Seurre he had prevented a disturbance by calling out to a gathering crowd, "Let honest men go to their homes; I only fire upon the mob." But his sympathies were with the principles of the Revolution; he was convinced that a new state of things could not come about without grave convulsions, and that it was impossible for any single man to oppose a great national movement. He was also of opinion that a new state of things might turn to the advantage of his beloved Corsica.

Another period of leave was due to Napoleon on 1 September 1789, and he was anxious to take advantage of it. Du Teil was very properly of opinion that no leave should be granted to officers in the present disturbed condition of affairs, urging that at Auxonne there were now only two or three captains instead of ten, and a dozen lieutenants instead of thirty. But Gouvernet, the governor of the province, objected that it would be dangerous to make unpopular innovations at the present juncture, and Du Teil did not insist. Indeed, he took leave himself, to look after his chateau in Dauphiné, which had been destroyed by the revolted peasants. In the case of Napoleon no objection was made; he received leave from 15 October 1789, to 1 June 1790, and, as was the rule with Corsican officers, was allowed to start a month earlier.

On his way Napoleon stopped at Valence and called on the Abbot of St Ruf, who said to him, "As things are going at present anyone may become king. If you become king, Monsieur de Bonaparte, make your peace with the Christian religion; you will find it advantageous." Napoleon replied that if he became king he would make the abbot a cardinal. Also a curious adventure befell him, which was a sign of the times. A noble lady travelled on the boat with him, accompanied by a young girl, also of noble birth. The lady had her carriage with her on the boat, and when she left the river she offered Napoleon a place in it. He refused, and asked if he might act as second courier, to save her the expense of a guide. When he took his leave of the lady, he said, "Will you believe that you were nearly arrested, and that I was the cause? You have a maid, a lady in waiting, and two couriers, one of whom is in uniform; you were taken for the Countess d'Artois on her way to the frontier, for you greatly resemble her." Napoleon embarked at Marseilles, where he paid a visit to the Abbé Raynal, whose acquaintance he had perhaps made in the previous year, and he reached Corsica in the last days of September.

CHAPTER VI

CORSICA

Napoleon arrived at Ajaccio at the end of September, 1789. He found the whole family assembled there, with the exception of Marianna, who was at the school of St Cyr. Joseph was a barrister; Lucien was doing nothing, being in weak health, and short-sighted; Louis was dependent upon his mother. Napoleon assumed the government of his family, and ruled them somewhat severely; but we are told that they enjoyed an exemplary character, and were regarded as one of the best conducted and the most united families in the town.

Corsica had sent four deputies to the States General at Versailles: Buttafuoco to represent the nobility, Peretti the clergy, and Saliceti and Colonna de Cesari Rocca to speak on behalf of the *tiers état*; the two first were aristocrats, the two latter democrats. The influence of the French Revolution began to be felt in the island, although Corsica had fewer grievances than France, because the nobility and the clergy were not privileged to the same extent. Their principal causes of complaint were the violence of the French officials, and the feebleness of the Corsican Estates, which had only a shadow of power. Rebellion against the *ancien régime* took the form of a desire either for independence, or for incorporation in the French monarchy.

At present the country was in an equivocal position. The Commander-in-Chief in Corsica at this time was the Vicomte de Barrin, a timid and irresolute man. He had only a few troops: six battalions and two companies of the Corps Royal, which were under their full strength. Barrin asked for further assistance, which was refused. He therefore had to temporize. He accepted the tricolour cockade given to him by the municipality of Bastia, and recommended the commandant of Ajaccio to do likewise. On the very day on which the soldiers of Ajaccio received the new emblem, 15 August 1789, the Fête of the Assumption and Napoleon's birthday, there was a revolt against the Archbishop Doria, which continued for several days. Similar outbreaks took place at Bastia, at Corte, and at Sartène. The news of these disturbances caused great agitation at Versailles. Saliceti, Cesari, and others, anxious to put an end to these disasters, established a national committee of twenty-two members, nominated according to population in different parts of the island. The committee was to receive reports from inspectors placed in each district, and send to Paris all necessary information for receiving and executing the decrees of the National Assembly. The troops were to assist the committee when required to do so, and a National Guard was to be formed in the island. These proposals were received in Corsica with enthusiasm, but they were opposed by Barrin and the aristocratic party, who feared the consequences of arming the people.

Such was the condition of Corsica when Napoleon returned full of patriotic fervour. He was determined to unmask the petty tyrants of his island, and to defend the cause of liberty; he was ambitious of taking a place amongst the heroes of his country, while Joseph was not less eager in the popular cause than his brother. He welcomed the Revolution with enthusiasm. He wrote a pamphlet entitled *Letters of Paoli to his Compatriots*, in which he showed how the Revolution was to regenerate Corsica. He was Corsican secretary of the committee of the thirty-six at Ajaccio. The two Bonapartes now joined together to play a conspicuous part in the public affairs of their island. Joseph had great designs; he desired first to enter the municipality of Ajaccio, then the departmental council, and thirdly the National Assembly at Paris. Napoleon assisted his elder brother by every means in his power, but they were too young to obtain the object of their desires, and Joseph found Pozzo di Borgo and Peraldi always standing in his way. Napoleon, on his arrival, warmly supported the project of a committee of twenty-two suggested by Saliceti and Cesari, while the French officials in Paris urged the employment of force. For this purpose, Gaffori, the father-in-law of Buttafuoco, was placed in command. He desired the restoration of order, and was opposed to the formation of the National Committee. He entered Ajaccio at the head of two hundred men of the Salis regiment, and five companies of the provincial regiment. His presence gave heart and courage to the friends of the *ancien régime*. He reviewed the garrison of the town and the troops which he had brought with him, and said that he would work day and night to repress all disorder. The National Guard was dissolved, much to the disgust of Napoleon, and the old committee of twelve pronounced against the formation of the new committee of twenty-two. The patriots of Bastia and Ajaccio both protested against this pronouncement of the twelve, on the ground that their conduct was tainted with despotism. Napoleon summoned the patriots of Ajaccio to a meeting in the church of St Francis, where he read them an address which he had drawn up, which he proposed to send to the National Assembly. He was indignant that the twelve should claim to represent the nation, when their only business was to decide on the land tax. He refuted the manifesto of the twelve point by point. He concluded by begging the National Assembly to restore to the Corsicans the rights which nature has given to every man. The address drawn up by Napoleon was soon covered with signatures, of which his own was the first. It was also signed by the Pozzo di Borgo, by the Archdeacon Lucien, and by Fesch.

At this time Bastia was roused to action by a letter from Saliceti, and Napoleon hastened thither to support the movement. He had many friends there, especially the Abbé Varese and the brothers Gallezzini. On the morning of 5 November 1789, the municipality of Bastia presented an address to Barrin, in which they asked for the formation of a civic guard. Barrin, after some delay, refused, and Rully, who was in command of the citadel, began to prepare it for the repression of the people, who were assembled in the Church of St John, At length the conflict broke out, and several were wounded on both sides. Barrin had entered the Church of St John to harangue the people, and was not permitted to come out. He was compelled to sign an order for arming the civic guard, and soon twelve hundred muskets passed into the hands of the citizens; upon which Barrin was set free. The people had conquered, and Rully was obliged to escape secretly. Other communes followed the example of Bastia. The condition of the island was reported by Saliceti to the National Assembly, and a decree was passed making Corsica an integral part of France, and placing it under the same constitution as the rest of the kingdom. The result of this was to make Corsica extremely popular in France as one of the principal homes of liberty. On receipt of the news, a *Te Deum* was chanted in all the churches of the island, and a bonfire was lighted at Ajaccio; whilst the people cried, "Evviva la Francia! Evviva il re!" And Napoleon hung out of the window of his palace a banner with the inscription, "Vive la nation! Vive Paoli! Vive Mirabeau!"

These events diverted Napoleon from his former hatred against France. France was now for him the home of liberty and the friend of his native land. He said, "She has opened her bosom to us, henceforth we have the same interests and the same solicitudes; it is the sea alone which separates us." He abandoned the idea of publishing the Corsican letters, and his new enthusiasm was shared by those who had up to the present time been partakers of his plans. At the same time the island remained in a disturbed condition. Committees were formed on all sides which claimed to command the National Guard and even the troops of the line. The national militia had no order or discipline: all those present demanded muskets, and walked about firing them off with blank cartridges; the country was in a state of anarchy. In these movements Napoleon took an active part. He succeeded in getting his brother Joseph elected a member of the Municipal Council although he was three years below the proper age, which was twenty-five.

At this time Napoleon entered into a close connection with Filippo Buonarotti and Filippo Masseria. The first of these was a Tuscan, who published at Bastia a paper entitled *Giornale Politico*, to which both Joseph and Napoleon were contributors. Massaria, a native of Ajaccio, entered the English service, and was the friend and confidant of Paoli. These friends took an active part in establishing a "Comité Superieur," which sat at Bastia from 2 March to 1 September 1790. It was illegal, but undoubtedly did good service in quieting and restraining the people. Unfortunately a quarrel broke out between the two capitals of Corsica, Bastia and Ajaccio, separated by a lofty chain of mountains, known locally by the appellation of Di quà and Di là. At a later period Napoleon was in favour of allowing this dualism to exist, but in 1790 he was an ardent partisan of unity. The question reached an acute stage when the Comité Superieur determined to meet at Orezza on 12 April. Ajaccio first resolved to send no representatives; but in consequence of a caucus held at the Bonaparte house this decision was reversed, and twelve deputies were chosen, amongst them Joseph Bonaparte, Massaria, and Pozzo di Borgo. Napoleon, although not a deputy, accompanied his brother to Orezza. The Committee sat from 12 to 20 April, and Gaffori was invited to be present. He succeeded in securing that the committee should meet in future at Corte, in the centre of the island. On 16 April Napoleon wrote to his colonel for a prolongation of leave, alleging that he could not join his regiment before 15 October, because of his state of health, which compelled him to drink the waters of Orezza. He forwarded a medical certificate, and received an additional leave of four months and a half without deduction of pay. Leave was given very easily in those days, but it is more probable that he did not desire to leave Corsica in the present crisis than that his health was really impaired. The delay enabled him to receive Paoli on his return to the island. A deputation sent from Ajaccio, of which Joseph Bonaparte formed part, met the aged general at Lyons. Paoli received Joseph in a friendly spirit, and presented him with a drawing which Charles Bonaparte had once made of him on a playing-card at Corte.

In the meantime the island was given up to anarchy. There was a conflict everywhere between the royal authorities and the municipalities, and Napoleon took the side of the latter. He set himself especially against La Ferandière, who commanded the citadel of Ajaccio. He demanded that he should submit himself to the orders of the municipality, that the cannon of the fortress should not be directed towards the town, and that the town militia should garrison the citadel, with the regular troops. This was an echo of the capture of the Bastille. On 17 July 1790 Paoli entered the harbour of Bastia; his journey through France had been a prolonged ovation. At Lyons, Tournon, Valence, Aix, Marseilles, and Toulon the populace had thronged around him with cries of "Vive Paoli!" Nor was his entry into his own country less imposing. He was a tall man, now sixty-six years of age, with piercing eyes and long white hair; everyone desired to see him and to touch him. He was met with salvos of artillery and cries of "Vive le père de la patrie!" His first step was to get rid of Gaffori and his regiment of Salis-Grisons. Napoleon lost no time in attaching himself to him, nor was Joseph less devoted. Another meeting, attended by 419 electors, was held at Orezza from 9 to 27 September. Paoli presided; and both Bonapartes were present, Joseph being an elector. The business was to elect members for the department; but, like the similar meeting of electors at Paris, it did a number of illegal things, which may, however, have been of general utility. Joseph, in spite of the efforts of Napoleon, was not elected deputy; indeed, he was not yet twenty-two years of age, and had not reached the age even to be an elector.

At this moment Napoleon's leave expired, and he was only waiting for a favourable wind to embark. On 16 November the municipality and the directory of Ajaccio passed a resolution that Napoleon possessed the character and the qualities of an honest citizen, that he was animated by the purest patriotism, that since the outbreak of the Revolution he had given reiterated and indubitable proofs of his attachment to the Constitution, that he had not been afraid to expose himself to the resentment of the vile flatterers and partisans of aristocracy, and that his countrymen viewed his departure with the most sincere regret. On the eve of his departure, 11 October 1790, he wrote a letter to Pozzo di Borgo full of denunciations of a certain Ponte, who had objected to the election of Joseph as President of the Directory of Ajaccio. Ponte's home, he said, was the centre of all their intrigue. Ponte had urged the people of Ajaccio to throw the bust of Paoli into the sea; Ponte had spread the report that the new lazaret was to be established at Saint Florentin, and not at Ajaccio, and he recommended the illegal dismissal of those from whom he disagreed; such an evil effect had party passion produced upon his usually calm and equable character. Driven back to the coast of Corsica by adverse winds, he opened at Ajaccio on 6 January 1791, a club called the Globo Patriotico, of which Joseph, Fesch, and Massaria were members, and which was of a very radical character. Whilst he remained at Ajaccio he was the soul of the society.

His last act was to write the *Letter to Buttafuoco*, who had attacked Paoli in the National Assembly, where he represented the Corsican nobility. Buttafuoco was at this moment even more unpopular than Gaffori. He was burned in effigy by the municipality of Ajaccio. Napoleon wrote his letter as the mouthpiece of the Globo, and it is dated Milelli, 25 January 1791. It is an eloquent philippic, full of fiery denunciation. It opens thus: "Sir, from Bonifacio to Cape Corso, from Ajaccio to Bastia, there is one chorus of imprecation against you. Your friends hide themselves; your relations disown you; and the wise man who never allows himself to be overcome by popular opinion is on this occasion carried away by the general excitement. What, then, have you done? What are the crimes which can justify so universal an indignation, so complete an abandonment? It is that, sir, which I am anxious to discover in explaining myself with you." He goes on to praise Paoli, his resources, his finance, his eloquence. He recalls the difficulties which the French experienced in conquering the island, he denounces the government of the King, and laments the destiny of his fellow-countrymen. He says that Corsica before 1789 was a nest of tyrants, a hideous country, which, crowded with victims and still reeking with the blood of martyrs, inspires at every step ideas of vengeance. He then turns to the career of Buttafuoco, and, in tracing it, reviews the history of Corsica from 1769-1790, and he concludes thus: "O Lameth! O Robespierre! O Pétion! O Volney! O Mirabeau! O Barnave! O Bailly! O Lafayette! this is the man who dares to set himself at your side; all dripping with the blood of his brothers, defiled by crimes of every kind, he presents himself with confidence in the garb of a general, the wicked recompense of his misdeeds. He loves to make himself the representative of a nation, a nation which he has sold, and you allow it. If it is the voice of the people, he never had any vote but that of the twelve nobles; if it is the voice of the people, Ajaccio and Bastia and the majority of the cantons have done to his effigy what they would like to have done to himself."

The letter was received with enthusiasm by the Globo, and ordered to be printed; but Paoli was less enthusiastic. He wrote to Napoleon, "Do not take the trouble to expose the impostures of Buttafuoco. His very relations are ashamed of him; leave him to the contempt and the indifference of the public." In 1801 the brother of Mlle Bou, who was selling his house, found some copies of the letter, and sent them to the First Consul; but he remarked, "These pamphlets have no object; they should be burnt."

CHAPTER VII

AUXONNE AND VALENCE

Napoleon, on his return to France, took with him his brother Louis, who was now twelve years and a half old, having been born on 2 September 1778. He stopped at Valence to visit some old friends. From the village of Serves, about four miles from St Vallier, he wrote to Fesch, whom he informs of the condition of political opinion in that part of France. In this letter he makes the suggestion that the Patriotic Society of Ajaccio should present Mirabeau with a complete suit of Corsican clothing, cap, vest, breeches, stockings, cartridge-case, stiletto, pistol, and musket, in compensation, apparently, for his having been threatened with a knife by Peretti, one of the Corsican deputies. At St Vallier he writes some reflections on love. "What, then, is love? The feeling of his weakness with which a solitary and isolated man is soon penetrated, the sentiment at once of his impotence and his immortality; the soul concentrates itself, doubles itself, fortifies itself, the delicious tears of passion flow—this is love." Then, looking at Louis, who sits before him, he continues, "Observe the young man, thirteen years of age—he loves his friend as he will love his mistress at twenty. Egoism is of later birth. At forty a man loves his fortune, at eighty himself."

He passed through Châlons on 9 February 1791, and excused himself for not calling on James, who had been a close friend of his brother Joseph at Autun; he, however, promoted him in later years. He arrived at Auxonne on 11 or 12 February, having considerably exceeded his leave, and being subject to lose his pay for three months and a half. He brought with him certificates from the Directory of the district of Ajaccio, which said not only that his patriotism was above suspicion, but that he had done his best to return to his duty at the proper time, but had been prevented by stress of weather. His colonel, M. de Lance, not only gave him a good reception, but asked that the pay which he had lost by his absence, amounting to nearly £10, should be made up to him. This request was acceded to by the Minister of War. His fellow-officers, who held royalist opinions, were not equally indulgent, and accused him of revolutionary conduct, against which he defended himself to the best of his ability.

Napoleon tells us that during his second sojourn at Auxonne he worked habitually fifteen or sixteen hours a day. He lived in a modest lodging, occupying a single room with an adjoining cabinet in which Louis slept. He gave his brother lessons in mathematics and did not spare corporal chastisements, although he was very fond of him. He was very proud of him, and said that he had both application and judgment, that he was a charming and an excellent fellow, and that he would be the most distinguished of the sons of Madame Letizia, as having had the best education. He writes, "Louis writes as much from inclination as from self-respect, and is full of sentiment; all he needs is knowledge. He has acquired a bright French manner. He goes into society, salutes with grace, and converses with a serious dignity which would become a man of thirty. All the women are in love with him." Their lodging was poorly furnished with a bed without curtains, a table in the window covered with books and papers, and two chairs, while Louis slept on a mattress.

Stories are current of the extreme poverty of Napoleon at this time, and of the sacrifices which he made for the sake of his brother. Undoubtedly he did make sacrifices, and he complained of his brother's ingratitude at a later period, reminding him how in his early youth he had deprived himself for his sake even of the necessaries of life. But we must not suppose that he led a morose or solitary life. He found amongst his fellow-officers Desmazis and other old companions, and made new acquaintances in the Suremain family, whom he afterwards did not forget. He also printed at Dôle a hundred copies of his letter to Buttafuoco, and walked there and back with Louis to correct the proofs. Nor did he forget his family. He urged them to pay the twelve crowns which Joseph owed to Buonarotti, and to complete the business of the *pepinière*. He also advised Lucien to get employment in a public office. He always had the courage of his opinions, and never hesitated to declare his adhesion to the principles of the Revolution. He told his publisher, Joly, that he would never serve any cause but that of liberty. One day some of his fellow-officers were so exasperated with him that they attempted to throw him into the Saône. When he heard that they were in danger of being arrested for this, he warned them and enabled them to escape. Amongst his friends at Auxonne he lauded the decrees of the National Assembly, and spoke with enthusiasm about the friendly connection between the army and the National Guard, and the fusion between the soldiers and the people. He even proposed to organize a civic festival at Auxonne, and to unite the National Guard and the regiment of La Fère in a monster banquet. In a visit which he paid to Nuits to visit his friend Gassendi, who had lately married, he had to maintain his democratic opinions almost single-handed against the rest of the company.

In 1791 the organization of the artillery was entirely changed by a decree of the National Assembly. This arm was separated from the infantry. The regiments lost their former names and were henceforth designated by numbers, La Fère becoming the first regiment. Each regiment had two battalions, each containing six companies. The sappers and the bombardiers disappeared, and all were known as gunners and cannoniers. The lieutenants *en premier* and the lieutenants *en seconde* became first and second lieutenants, the lieutenants *en troisième* disappeared. Bonaparte, instead of lieutenant *en seconde*, became first lieutenant. The officers with new names were distributed amongst the different regiments, and Napoleon was appointed first lieutenant of the Fourth Regiment, known formerly as the Regiment de Grenoble, now in garrison at Valence. His pay was £4 a month. He did not like the change, and endeavoured to keep his old position, but his request came too late, and he left Auxonne on 14 June 1791. He never forgot his friends in the town or his old regiment of La Fère. On 4 June 1802, he said to them at Paris, "Officers and soldiers of the First Regiment of Foot Artillery, it was in your regiment that I acquired the first lessons of the art of war; I have always noticed that your regiment is obedient to the sentiments of honour and fame; be worthy of being the first in the first division of the army." Even so late as 14 May 1815, he recognized by sight a man who had been bombardier of his company in the regiment of La Fère, and brought tears to his eyes, and there are many examples of the same kind.

Napoleon arrived at Valence on 16 June and was attached to the first company of the second battalion. He lived in his old lodgings, in the house of Mlle Bou, with his brother close by him. Louis boarded with the landlady, who looked after him like a mother, but Napoleon took his meals at the Three Pigeons. He renewed his relations with his former friends. Louis had as companion one François, the son of a lawyer, Mésangère Cleyrac. With a gratitude worthy of his brother he never forgot him, but made him the treasurer of the House of Holland, and manager of his property in France. The Abbé de Saint Ruf was dead, but Madame de Colombier and her daughter were living, as before, in their country house at Basseaux, where Napoleon was a frequent visitor, and where he introduced Louis. He made two new friends, Sucy and Bachasson de Montalivet, whom he never forgot. In 1801 Montalivet spent the day with him at Malmaison. The First Consul asked him the most minute questions about the friends whom he had known at Valence, and eventually about a woman who kept a coffee shop. On hearing that she was still alive, Napoleon said that he was afraid that he might not have paid her for all the cups of coffee which he had drunk in her house, and sent her fifty louis as a present. Comte de Montalivet became Minister of the Interior in 1809, and was Intendant General de la Couronne during the Hundred Days, a Membre de la Chambre des Pairs. Sucy, whom he called his dear old friend, and employed in Italy and in Egypt, said of him, in 1797, that he would end either on the throne or on the scaffold.

Napoleon was an ardent supporter of the Revolution, and did not frequent the drawing-rooms where the tone was mainly aristocratic. If the Revolution was not fashionable, it was extremely popular. A Society of the Friends of the Constitution met in the house of Mlle Bou. Of this Napoleon became a member on his arrival, and made a speech of such eloquence that he was nearly chosen as president, notwithstanding his youth. The common soldiers were on the side of the nation, but the officers were for the most part aristocrats.

Four days after Napoleon's arrival at Valence there took place what was perhaps the most important incident of the Revolution, the flight to Varennes. The result of this was that the Constituent Assembly ordered all the officers in the army to take an oath of allegiance to it: swearing to maintain the Constitution against all enemies both within and without, to die rather than suffer the invasion of French territory by foreign troops, to obey no orders but those given in pursuance of the decrees of the Assembly. This oath had to be written by each officer with his own hand, and signed by him. This important duty was executed by Napoleon on 6 July 1791. There is no doubt that Napoleon was at this time a Republican. He often discussed politics with Sucy and Montalivet. Sucy was a royalist, Montalivet was in favour of a constitutional monarchy, but Bonaparte asserted that a republic was the only logical form of government; that a nation freely constituted always knew what was best for itself; that the French would never be really free till they got rid of their king. The arguments of the royalists only strengthened him in his opinions; he said that they took great pains to bolster up a bad cause, and that in declaring that monarchy was the best form of government they asserted what was incapable of proof.

The necessity of taking the oath to the Constituent Assembly produced a profound effect in the army. Many officers refused at once to have anything to do with it; others took it with a mental reservation and afterwards emigrated. Like burning political questions in our own time, it broke up the ties of family life. Brother was divided against brother. The famous Desaix joined the new regime, whereas his two brothers remained faithful to the lily. No less than thirty-two officers of the fourth regiment refused to serve under a republic. But Napoleon disapproved of this step, which placed the king above the nation, and it was a fixed principle with him that everything should be sacrificed to the country. At the same time, in later life he did not lose his interests in his former comrades, and if they chose to return from emigration he received them kindly. His relations with one of them, Hédouville, are worth recording. Hédouville and Serurier were crossing the frontier into Spain, when they were stopped by a French patrol. Hédouville, being younger and more active, escaped, and led a miserable life in a foreign country. Serurier was stopped, and became a marshal of France. When Hédouville returned to France he was appointed by the First Consul *aide-de-camp* to his brother. In public Napoleon received him coldly, but when they were left alone, he pulled his ear, and said, "Good day, Chevalier; where do you come from?" "I come from Spain," was the answer.

"You were an *emigré*," said the Emperor. Hédouville was silent. "You know how to lie," said Napoleon; "I will employ you in diplomacy." He was attached to the legation at Rome, and afterwards became Minister at Ratisbon and at Frankfurt. At a later time, from his knowledge of Spanish, he was very useful to Joseph, who always found him perfectly loyal. Once when Hédouville was present at an audience, Napoleon pointed him out to the assembly, and said, "There is one of my old comrades, with whom I have broken many a lance, on the Place des Clercs at Valence, in discussing the Constitution of 1791. I was in favour of the suspensive veto, Hédouville of the absolute veto; and I recognize now that he was right." To talk military "shop" was forbidden at Valence, under payment of a fine, and Napoleon had to pay the largest penalty; but politics occupied a large portion of his interests, and he was so outspoken in his views that some of his comrades would not speak to him, and others would not sit next to him at table. Napoleon, however, returned good for evil. On 25 August, the *fête* of Saint Louis, Du Prat, who had told the servants in Napoleon's hearing never to place him next to Bonaparte, was standing at the window of the Three Pigeons, and singing Grétry's air, "O Richard, O mon roi." He was nearly lynched by the people, and was only saved by Napoleon's intervention.

We have said that Napoleon, on his arrival at Valence, joined the club of the Friends of the Constitution, and that he was put forward for the presidency. He was elected librarian and secretary. The club numbered two hundred members, and was affiliated to the Jacobin Club at Paris on 3 July 1791, when there was a great meeting of democratic clubs at Valence. They met at seven a.m., heard Mass in the cathedral, after which they repaired to the disused church of St Ruf. As was the custom in those times, all those present took an oath to be faithful to the nation and to the law, to maintain the Constitution at the peril of their lives, to rally round the banner of liberty, to watch over the enemies of the republic, and to defend with their fortune and their blood anyone who had the courage to denounce traitors. Then, by a spontaneous movement, they all took the same oath which had been taken by the officers. Then followed speeches and a collection for patriotic purposes.

The events of this day made a profound impression on Napoleon. He was fired by the enthusiasm of his own soldiers, one of whom cried, in the name of his comrades, "We have common heart and aims; we owe them to the Constitution." The inviolability of the king was discussed, and the assembly determined unanimously that all citizens were subject to the law. They also signed a petition that the king should be brought to judgment.

On 14 July, the anniversary of the capture of the Bastille, the civic oath was taken in the Champ de l'Union, the bishop officiating at the altar, and the *Veni Creator* being sung. After the Mass shouts of "I swear" were heard, mingled with the roar of cannon and the strains of "Ça ira," played by the band, a strange Mezentian marriage of the living and the dead. A banquet was afterwards held, at which Napoleon proposed the health of the patriots of Auxonne, and of all those who in that city defended the rights of the people. Naudin, Napoleon's correspondent in that town, founded there a club of the Friends of the Revolution, which was affiliated to the Jacobin Club at Paris. On 27 July Napoleon writes to him at the close of the day, to calm his brain before he went to bed: "Will there be war? I have always said no, for the following reasons:—The sovereigns of Europe reign either over men or over cattle and horses. The first, such as England and Holland, understand the Revolution, but are afraid of it; the second understand it, and believe that it will bring about the ruin of France. Therefore they will do nothing, but will wait for the civil war, which they believe inevitable, to break out. This country is full of zeal and fire. The southern blood which flows in my veins courses with the rapidity of the Rhône; pardon me, therefore, if you have some difficulty in deciphering my scrawl."

During these political excitements Napoleon did not neglect his studies, as we know from the evidence of his notebooks. He made an abstract of

Coxe's book on Switzerland, paying special attention to the government of the cantons, and was able to tell the Swiss deputies in 1802 that he had studied the geography and the manners of their country. He read the Florentine History of Machiavelli in a translation, and the memoirs of Duclos on the Courts of Louis XIV., the regency, and Louis XV. He also made notes on the *Histoire Critique de le Noblesse* by M. Dulaure. The extracts which he made from these books are very characteristic; they have generally some practical application, and show a deeply seated passion for good government. Another abstract, which throws light on his relations with the Papacy, is that of *L'Esprit de Gerson* by Eustache L. Noble. In this he clearly distinguishes between the spirit of ultramontanism and that of Gallicanism. The nineteenth notebook contains explanations of words and terms in ancient and modern history, which show his diligence and his curiosity. The entries extend from 10 April to 1 August 1791. A notebook of nine pages written in May, 1791, contains an abstract of the first volume of Voltaire's *Essai des mœurs*. A short essay, written probably immediately after the king's flight, discussing the comparative merit of a monarchy or a republic, begins with the words, "My tastes have led me for a long time to interest myself in public affairs. If an unprejudiced publicist can have any doubt as to the preference which should be given to republicanism over monarchism, I think that today his doubts will be removed." These notes show that Napoleon was not only a student, but a thinker; they bear the mark of an intense individuality.

The Academy of Lyons had announced that in 1791 it would give a prize for the best essay on the following subject: "What truths and what sentiments is it most important to impress upon men for their happiness." This prize, which was worth about £50, had been founded by the Abbé Raynal, and he had probably advised Napoleon to be a candidate for it.

Napoleon had discussed the subject of the essay with his brother Joseph during his stay at Ajaccio, and from February 1791, he was haunted by the question, "In what does happiness consist?" It was this feeling which made him write his reflections on "love," of which we have already spoken. He also read carefully the essay of Rousseau, which gained the prize at the Academy of Dijon on the origin and foundation of inequality, and in reading it he criticized it severely. He ended by stating his own ideas, which are indeed full of truth, and elevated truth, that man had from the very first the faculties of reason and of sentiment, that he desired society and love, and that primeval man was capable of feeling pity, friendship, love, and also gratitude and respect. He concludes that unless reason and sentiment were inherent qualities of man, virtue would neither be a duty nor a pleasure.

He begins his essay by defining happiness as the enjoyment of a life which is most suited to our organization. But our organization is two-fold—animal and intellectual—one as strong as the other. Our intellectual appetites are as imperious as our animal appetites, and happiness cannot be possible without their complete development. Sentiment and reason are qualities peculiar to man, they are his titles to the supremacy which he has acquired, which he preserves and which he will always preserve. It is sentiment that is the source of our activity, which makes us friends of the noble and the just, and enemies of the oppressor and the villain. In sentiment lies conscience, the source of morality. Reason is the judge, the censor of our actions, and should be their invariable rule. Reason saves men from the precipice of passion, and tempers in him the desire to press his rights. Society has its origin in sentiment, and its support in reason. A man to be happy must eat, sleep, beget children, but he must also have sentiment and reason. He then makes the somewhat strange remark that of all legislators, the two who have most strongly apprehended these truths are Lycurgus and Monsieur Paoli. He begins by introducing to us a young man asking for advice in the conduct of life. The priest says, "Do not reflect on the existence of society. God directs everything; abandon yourself to His providence." A lawyer tells him that happiness is divided amongst individuals according to law. His father advises him to be content with his lot: "Be a man, but be one in all truth, live master of yourself; without strength, my son, there is no virtue nor happiness. Still, it is only just that the poorest should possess something. Paoli has done more than any other legislator to effect this." He then concludes, "The law should assure to everyone his physical existence, the thirst for wealth is to give place to the consoling sentiment of happiness, and the barbarous law of primogeniture is to be abolished, and children are to share their father's property equally; man is to learn that his true glory is to live like a man, that he is to marry, which will be the triumph of morality. These are the views which should be inculcated for a happy life."

In the second part he asks, "What is sentiment? It is the bond of life, of society, of love, and of friendship. It unites the son to the mother, the citizen to his country. It is blunted by sensuality, but revived by misfortune." "Climb one of the peaks of Mont Blanc, see the sun, gradually rising, bring consolation and hope to the cottage of the labourer; let its first ray be received into your heart, remember the sensation which it gives you. See the sun set on the sea, melancholy will overcome you, you will abandon yourself to it, the melancholy of nature cannot be resisted. Stand beneath some Roman monument, your imagination will move in distant ages with Æmilius, Scipio, and Fabius; you will see the plain where a hundred thousand Cimbri lie buried. The Rhône flows in the far distance, swifter than an arrow, there is a road on the left, the little town of Tarascon is not far off, flocks pasture in the meadows, you dream, doubtless—it is the dream of sentiment. Sleep in the hut of a shepherd, lying on skins, a fire at your feet, midnight sounds, the herds are led forth to pasture: what a moment to enter into yourself and to meditate on the origin of nature in tasting the most delicious pleasures! Thus also the silence of the starlit night after the fierce heat of a summer's day, the calm reflection of a solitary evening after your family have retired to rest, a night spent alone in some great cathedral, a tent life on the island of Monte Cristo, under the wall of a ruined monastery, lulled by the roaring of the waves breaking on the rocks. All these situations will fill you with sentiment."

The stress which Napoleon lays on the importance of sentiment to the character, of its universality, and its intimate connection with the rest of a man's nature is surely very remarkable, and comes from his deepest heart. But listen to this: "You return to your country after four years of absence, you visit the sites where you played in your earliest age, where you first experienced the knowledge of men and the awakening of the passions. In a moment you live the life of your childhood, you enjoy its pleasures, you are fired with the love of your country, you have a father and a tender mother, sisters still innocent, brothers who are like friends; too happy man, run, fly, do not lose a moment. If death stop you on your way you will never have known the delights of life, of sweet gratitude, of tender respect, of sincere friendship. These are the real pleasures of life, and they are greater if you have a wife and children. If your soul was as burning as the furnace of Etna; if you have a father, a wife and children, you never need be afraid of the weariness of life. Thus, by sentiment we enjoy ourselves, nature, our country, and the men who surround us."

Napoleon's views on music are interesting. "Music is born with man; music is at once a gift of sentiment and a means of regulating it. At every age, in every situation—even amongst animals—music consoles, rejoices, and gives an agreeable excitement. To the piping of the little bird the labourer joins his rustic voice, his soul expands, and, whether he is singing his loves, his desires, or his woes, his work, or the burden of labours, he finds himself refreshed. Do not let us, therefore, proscribe music—that tender companion of emotional man, the inspirer of sentiment. Let it increase the number of our pleasures, and, in tasting by degrees the charms of melody, let man convince himself more fully of the delights of sentiment, of the happiness of a country life, of the innocence of the earliest ages."

The third part is devoted to the examination of reason, also, according to Napoleon, an inherent equality of man. "Reason is perfection by means of logic, logic is the faculty which leads us to compare. Some truths are apprehended by sentiment, others by logic. There is a universal logic, common to all natures and to all ages." After discussing how reason is to be bought, and admitting that he does not desire to have lectures on Euclid in every cottage, he diverges to a praise of liberty, which he seems to regard as the product of reason and logic. "Without liberty there is no energy, no virtue, no strength in nations; without energy, without virtue, without strength, there is no sentiment, no natural reason, there is no happiness. All tyrants will doubtless go to hell; but their slaves will go there also, for after the crime of oppressing a nation, the crime of suffering oppression is the most monstrous. Let these principles be incessantly repeated to men. To resist oppression is their fairest right, that which tyrants fear most, and they have always been afraid of it. After the lapse of ages, the Frenchman, brutalized by kings and their ministers, by nobles and their prejudices, by priests and their impostures, has suddenly awakened and traced out the Rights of Man. Let them serve as a rule to the legislator." Napoleon's remarks upon ambitions are very curious. "The lover grown to manhood is mastered by ambition—ambition, with pale complexion, wandering eyes, hurried gait, irregular gestures, sardonic smile. Crimes are his playthings: intrigue is but a means; falsehood, calumny, backbiting but an argument, a figure of elocution. He arrives at the helm of affairs: the homage of people wearies him; but he can do good. What can be more consoling to the nerves than to say, 'I have just assured the happiness of a hundred families; I gave myself trouble, but the State will go the better for it; my fellow-citizens live more quietly by my want of rest, are more happy by my perplexities, and more gay by my sorrows'? The man who desires to succeed only from the wish to contribute to the public happiness, is the virtuous man who feels that he possesses courage, firmness, and talents. He will master his ambition instead of being mastered by it, will enjoy both sentiment and reason; he always enjoys most liberty. But ambition, the immoderate desire to satisfy pride or intemperance—which is never satisfied—which leads Alexander from Thebes to Persia, from Granicus to Issus, from Issus to Arbela, and thence to India—ambition, which causes him to conquer and to ravage the world without being able to satisfy it, the same flame consumes him; in his delirium he knows not where to direct it, he becomes agitated, he is led astray. Alexander believes himself a god, he believes himself the son of Jupiter, and wishes to make others believe it. The ambition which leads the merchant to fortune, and then to be Controleur-Général, without his being contented with the first place in the finances; the ambition which guided Cromwell as he guided England, but to torment him with all the daggers of the Furies; the ambition which overturns states and private families, which is fed upon blood and crime; the ambition which inspired Charles V, Philip II, Louis XIV, is, like all disordered passions, a violent unreflecting madness, which only ceases with life—a conflagration, fanned by a pitiless wind, which does not end till it has consumed everything." And again, "The tempests of the ocean are preferable to its stagnation, which makes its exhalations fatal. Passion is preferable to absolute stupidity, to degrading libertinage. Better be an enthusiast, a man of passions, than a man without sensibility. Doubtless we should prefer the delirium of sentiment to its slumber or its death. Do you know what is the cause of disordered passions? The prevention of natural enjoyment. Deprived of these the fire of sentiment has no vent; it ferments and produces passion, and the imagination, the true box of Pandora, receptacle of all vices, deranges all a man's appetites. Men, live conformably to your nature, feel and reason according to sentiment and natural reason, and you will be happy!"

There is no doubt that Napoleon put his whole soul into this essay, and that anyone who wishes to understand what he was at twenty-two should read it with attention. But he did not gain the prize. Sixteen essays were sent in, Napoleon's having the number 15. The examiner pronounced that it was too ill-arranged, too unequal, too vague, and too badly written to merit attention. The Academy decided to adjourn the awarding of the prize for two years, and only gave an honourable mention to No. 8. This was written by Daunou, the well-known historian, who, after revising his essay, gained the prize with it in 1793. Bonaparte's essay offers a psychological study of the most interesting character. How little did he know what was hidden in the depths of his own nature! This is what he says of the man of genius, "The unfortunate man! I pity him. He will be the admiration and the envy of his contemporaries, and the most miserable of all. His equilibrium is broken, he will live unhappy. Ah! the fire of genius—but let us not alarm ourselves—it is so rare. What years pass without Nature producing a genius! Men of genius are meteors destined to burn for the illumination of their age."

CHAPTER VIII

AJACCIO

Having finished his essay, Napoleon determined to ask for further leave. The inactivity of a garrison was weariness to him, and his family had need of him. His request was refused by Colonel Campagnol, but Napoleon determined to apply directly to the Baron du Teil, who had commanded the School at Auxonne and was now Inspector-General of Artillery for that part of France. He therefore paid him a visit at his Château of Pommier, in the department of the Isère. He was received with great kindness, and stayed in the house several days discussing the art of war and a possibility of a new road from France to Italy. When he left, Du Teil said of him, "He is a man of great powers, and will make a name." Eventually, he obtained permission of absence and was allowed to keep his pay, but was ordered to rejoin his regiment in November, after a lapse of three months. He reached Corsica, together with his brother Louis, in September, 1791. On 15 October, his great-uncle Lucien, head of his house, and a second father to him, died. He said on his deathbed to his niece, "Letizia, do not cry; I die content because I see you surrounded by all your children, my life is no longer necessary to them; Joseph is at the head of the administration of the country, and can manage your affairs. Your Napoleon will be a great man, *un omone*." He also recommended Letizia to defer in important matters to the advice of her second son. Napoleon undertook the direction of the family, brothers and sisters obeyed him without objection. Louis says that they never discussed with him; he was angry at the least observation, and got into a passion at the slightest resistance. The Archdeacon left a considerable sum of money. At the close of the year Napoleon, in conjunction with Fesch, bought the house of La Trabocchina, in the town of Ajaccio, and two properties, Saint Antonio and Vignale, in the suburbs.

At this time, Paoli was master of the island; he was Commander-in-Chief of the National Guards and President of the administration of the department. All power was thus concentrated in his hands, and his position had been strengthened by having put down the revolt of Bastia. In the last fortnight of September, three hundred and forty-six electors assembled at Corte to elect six deputies for the new Legislative Assembly at Paris, to nominate the juries for the High Court of Orleans, to determine the capital of the department and the seat of the bishopric. The six deputies elected were, generally speaking, friends of Paoli and included Pozzo di Borgo and Marius Peraldi. Corte was chosen for the capital, and Ajaccio for the seat of the bishopric. Joseph Bonaparte was not even nominated for the post of deputy, but he was elected with seven others to the executive committee called the Directory, although he was only twenty-three years of age. His office compelled him to reside at Corte. Napoleon himself came to Corte in February, 1792, where he met for the first time the famous Volney, to whom he became so much attached. Volney was anxious to introduce the culture of cotton, and for that purpose bought the estate of Confina del Principe, which he called his "little India." He became a citizen of Ajaccio, and talked of founding a newspaper which should be bought by all the communes of the island. Volney and Napoleon seemed to have been equally anxious to make each other's acquaintance. Writing to Sucy on 17 February 1792, Napoleon says of him, "M. de Volney is known in the republic of letters by his travels in Egypt, by his essay on Agriculture, by his political and commercial discussions on the Treaty of '56, by his meditation on the Ruins, and is equally well known in patriotic annals by his firmness in supporting the good cause in the Constituent Assembly." Napoleon made the tour of the island with Volney, and probably advised him to purchase the property of La Confina. It is interesting to reflect what Volney must have told him of Egypt and of the power of the Mamelukes, who kept the population in serfdom, and how little Volney can have suspected that he was conversing with one of those conquerors whom he abhorred. Napoleon was already under the spell of the past, and had read the Ancient History of Rollin, and the history of the Arabs by Marigny.

At the same time the ambition of Napoleon was to be appointed adjutant-major of the volunteers, the post being in the gift of Antonio Rossi, who was the deputy of General Biron, commandant of the island. He was a distant cousin of the Bonapartes, and finding it difficult to procure competent adjutant-majors, was glad enough to request the ministry to give the post to Bonaparte. Rossi expected to receive an immediate answer, but it did not arrive, and in the meantime, a law of 11 December 1791 enjoined that the troops of all the garrisons of France should be passed under review between 25 December 1791 and 10 January 1792, and that any officer who was found to be absent should be deprived of his commission. Napoleon was afraid of falling between two stools. He therefore wrote to his friend Sucy on 17 February 1792, saying that he had been detained in Corsica by urgent private affairs, meaning the death of his great-uncle Lucien, asking what had taken place in the review of 10 January; had he been deprived of his commission, and, if so, how could he get back? He promised to return the moment he heard from Sucy, if Sucy advised him to do so. But on 14 January 1792, the National Minister of War replied that the nomination of Napoleon to the post of adjutant-major would be perfectly legal. On 22 February he was formally appointed Adjutant-Major of the Corsican Volunteers of Ajaccio, and Rossi notified this appointment to Colonel Campagnol.

In February 1792, Rossi received a law of the Legislative Assembly which provided that all officers employed in the volunteer battalions must rejoin their regiments before 1 April. He therefore informed Napoleon that he must surrender the post of adjutant-major. As, however, the law made an exception in favour of first and second lieutenant-colonels of national battalions, Napoleon determined to obtain the post of lieutenant-colonel of the second battalion of the Corsican volunteers, to which he had to be elected. He had five competitors, the most formidable of whom were Quenza and Pozzo di Borgo, Quenza being supported by Paoli. Napoleon made an arrangement with Quenza that they should unite against Pozzo di Borgo, that Quenza should be elected first lieutenant-colonel and Napoleon second, the Bonapartists, already an organized party, supporting Quenza, and Quenza nominating Napoleon. To obtain his object Napoleon exerted himself to the utmost. He was very young, only twenty-two, and he looked like a boy of fifteen. But his rank and uniform as an officer of artillery gave him influence, and he had on his side the assurance of his bearing, the firmness of his attitude, and the warmth and audacity of his speech. Pozzo di Borgo was supported by the Peraldi, who laughed at the ambitious and violent temper of Napoleon, at his small stature, and smaller fortune. Napoleon challenged Peraldi to a duel, but Napoleon awaited his antagonist till evening without his appearing. Napoleon, to the dismay of his careful mother, squandered the treasure of the Archdeacon in entertaining those who would be useful to him, and kept open house.

The Bonaparte mansion in the Rue St Charles was the rendezvous of the volunteers who were devoted to his cause; they slept on mattresses in the rooms and on the staircase. The election was to be held on 1 April, and the day before the three commissioners of the department who were to preside at the elections arrived at Ajaccio. Morati lodged with the Peraldi, Quenza with the Ramolini, and Grimaldi with the Bonapartes. Napoleon, after a day's reflection, sent a friend, Bonelli, to carry off Morati by force from the Peraldi and to bring him to the Rue St Charles. Napoleon said to him, "I desired that you should be free; you are not free with the Peraldi; here you are at home." This action seems to have been sufficiently in accordance with Corsican manners to excite no great surprise. Morati slept in the Bonapartes' house, and next day went to the meeting under their protection. The voting took place in the Church of St Francis. All the volunteers were present without uniform or arms, but the greater number carried pistols and daggers under their clothes. Matteo Pozzo protested against the violence of the day before, but he was first knocked down, then dragged by force from the tribune, and he would have been killed if Napoleon and Quilico Casanova had not protected him with their bodies. Quenza was elected lieutenant-colonel and Napoleon second lieutenant-colonel.

It is difficult, to criticize this transaction, because we do not know enough about Corsican manners and customs. It is possible that if Morati had stayed with the Peraldi Napoleon might have still been elected, but that disorders might have arisen which would have been equal to a civil war on a small scale. It is, at any rate, certain that Morati did not feel resentment at the manner in which he had been treated. At any rate, the result was obtained; the house in the Rue St Charles was full of joy. Lucien sent a letter to Joseph, "Napoleon is lieutenant-colonel with Quenza. At this moment the house is full of people, and the band of the regiment." But it disturbed for ever their relation with the Pozzo di Borgo and the Peraldi. Charles André Pozzo di Borgo, who afterwards became Russian Ambassador, and a bitter enemy of Napoleon, had up to this time been his friend. They had conversed together on the past and future of Corsica, on Montesquieu and Rousseau, on the superiority of republics to monarchies, but that was now for ever over, and the Peraldi never forgot the treatment of Matteo, which they attributed to Napoleon. A Corsican vendetta does not always settle itself with the stiletto, but works sometimes for a surer and more cruel form of vengeance, and this Pozzo found in Napoleon's fall.

As soon as he was elected Napoleon took the command, and made his authority felt. Quenza had no great experience in military affairs, and Napoleon managed the minutest details of the service. The battalion took the name of Quenza-Bonaparte. Mario Peraldi said, "Poor Quenza! here he is, enveloped in the designs of Bonaparte, and these new Agamemnons will render him the passive instrument of their will." Napoleon had taken the precaution of securing his retreat. If he had not been elected he would have joined his regiment, and presented a certificate from Rossi to excuse his absence. Rossi said in this that he required an officer who could speak Italian, that he had appointed him adjutant-major of the volunteers, that he had informed the colonel of the 4th regiment artillery of this, that on becoming acquainted with the law of 3 February he had begged Napoleon to join his regiment, but that communications were slow and uncertain, and that he could not return earlier. Napoleon now wished to go to Paris, it is not certain with what object, but Rossi made objections, and events occurred which gave his mind another direction.

Napoleon determined to establish, if possible, his volunteers in the citadel of Ajaccio. He had been led to form this resolution by the Directory, of which Joseph was a member, who desired that the strong places of the island, Bastia, Calvi, Ajaccio, Bonifacio, and Corte, should be held by volunteers instead of the royal troops occupying the strongholds, while the volunteers were dispersed throughout the country. Rossi objected to this step, but he was overruled by the Directory, and they were supported in this particular measure by Paoli, who wished "esser sicuro dei presidi," "to be sure of the fortresses." Therefore to place the Corsican volunteers in the citadel of Ajaccio was in accordance with Paoli's views. There was also another reason for dealing strongly with Ajaccio. The inhabitants were very devout, whereas the Directory were animated by the principles of the Revolution, and Saliceti, the Procureur-General Syndic, was determined to give effect to the decrees of the Assembly. On 7 May 1792, Joseph and the other members of the Directory wrote to the Minister of the Interior that the fanatical members no longer dared to show themselves; that the Corsicans were too ardently attached to liberty to be led astray by hypocrites; that the Department had interrupted the payment of the pensions of non-juring priests, in order to bring them to a better mind; and that there were not more than twenty-two nonconformists on the island. Fesch himself, who was now vicar-general, approved of the civil constitution of the clergy, and had taken the oath to the constitution; but the majority of the inhabitants regarded the non-jurors as their true pastors, and as alone qualified to say Mass.

Consequently there was great excitement in the town, when, at the close of 1791, it was reported that the convent of the Capuchins was about to be closed. Paoli said, "The devout ladies of the town wish to preserve these beards, so venerable and so agreeable." The Directory issued an order on 25 February 1792, for the suppression of the convents of Ajaccio, Bastia,

Bonifacio, and Corte. The Capuchins left Ajaccio on 25 March, and on the same day the municipal, administrative, and judicial bodies met in the Church of St Francis, and determined to send a deputation to Corte to beg the Directory to restore the Capuchins to their convent. Joseph replied to them, "Off with you! If M. Saliceti, who is absent, were to find you here, he would send you to the Castle prison, and those who sent you after you. Off with you at once! and do not make useless demands."

There were many considerations which compelled Napoleon to take strong measures. He could not bear that the priests should endeavour to set themselves above the law. On 1 March, the Directory wrote to Rossi that the presence of four companies of volunteers in Ajaccio was necessary to ensure the public tranquillity, and a few days later they entered the town. The battalion Quenza-Bonaparte was reviewed in the Place d'Armes on 2 April. The Ajaccio companies occupied the Seminary; the four companies from Tallano were separated, and were established, one in a house in the town, and the three others in a building, called the new barracks, outside the ramparts. All these preparations were very disturbing to the population. Some families emigrated to Italy; the old antagonism between town and country began to revive; the volunteers treated the people of Ajaccio as "cittadini;" the Ajaccians called the volunteers "paesani." At last an event occurred which set fire to the fuel already laid.

On Easter Day, 8 April 1792, some non-juring priests celebrated Mass in the convent of St Francis, and announced that a procession would take place on the following day. At about five o'clock in the evening some young girls, who were playing bowls, quarrelled, and two sailors, named Rocca and Tavera, became involved in the dispute. Tavera brandished his stiletto, but, being disarmed, appeared with a pistol. Suddenly a detachment of twelve volunteers, commanded by an officer named Tancredi, advanced from the Seminary barracks. They stopped a man who was carrying a pistol, and when he resisted, carried him off prisoner to the Seminary. The volunteers then stopped a master mason named Joachim Favella, and began to search him. Favella resisted, and his brother Battista came up with a pistol and discharged it at the National Guards. Tancredi shouted, "Fire!" The two Favellas were not hit, but artisans and sailors went to their aid. Three of the volunteers were disarmed, and a fourth was severely wounded. Tancredi led his men back to their quarters, the people firing at them from the windows.

Napoleon was at this time in the Grand Rue. He collected six or seven officers of the battalion and went towards the Seminary. But when he arrived at the Ternano house, which was close to the cathedral, he saw

Marianna Ternano all in tears, making signs that he should escape. Notwithstanding this, he advanced, and met a carpenter, Ignazio Sari, carrying two muskets in his hand. Captain Giovanni Peretti recognized the muskets as belonging to two soldiers of his company, and saying to Sari, "Give me these muskets," took one himself and gave the other to his lieutenant, Peretti. At this moment a relation of Sari, commonly called Bartinione, appeared on the steps of the cathedral. His wife gave him a musket, with which he aimed at the officers. Napoleon reasoned with him, and he laid his musket down. Then some of his friends came out of the cathedral, upon which Bartinione resumed his musket, aimed at the officers, fired, and shot Lieutenant Rocca Serra dead.

Bonaparte and his friends took refuge in the Ternano house, and regained the Seminary by a back way. In all the streets cries were raised of "Adosso alle berrette! Adosso alla spallette!" "Down with the birettas! Down with the epaulettes!" The populace were armed with muskets and daggers. They fired at the windows of Quenza's house, and on Captain Peretti, and committed other breaches of order. The Council General of the Commune met in the evening, and decided to seek out and to punish the guilty. The body of Rocca Serra had been carried into the cathedral, and an inquiry was held there during the night. Napoleon afterwards accused the municipality of inaction. He said, "They did not move; they did not beat the assembly, nor even hoist the red flag; and when night came on, the magistrates, whose duty it was to watch while the citizens slept, were asleep while everybody was awake."

Napoleon and Quenza certainly did not sleep. They took the side of the soldiers against the people. Napoleon obtained some ammunition from his own house in the Rue St Charles. He was in a strong position. The tower of the Seminary, which was joined to the fortifications, commanded the Rue de La Cathedrale and the Place d'Armes. Napoleon was anxious to avenge the death of Rocca Serra, and to chastise the partisans of the Capuchins. He also wished to gain possession of the citadel. On the very same night he went with Quenza to Colonel Maillard, and requested him to open to them the gate of the fortress. Maillard replied that he was forbidden to do this by law, without the order of the king or his ministers. Quenza and Bonaparte did not insist, but they begged Maillard at least to give them munitions of war. He replied that he had already given as much as had been ordered by Rossi, and that he could not go beyond his instructions. He consented, however, to supply them with some bread.

On the morning of Easter Monday, 9 April, Drago, the *juge de paix*, escorted by a company of gendarmes, came to the Seminary to ask if any of the wounded volunteers were there. Quenza and Bonaparte assured him that there were none, but when he turned to go away they ordered him to remain, as well as his gendarmes. He was assisted to escape in the afternoon. Just at this moment (seven o'clock in the morning) some volunteers broke into the tower of the Seminary and fired at the people who were coming out of the cathedral after the Mass. Two women were killed. Santo Peraldi, an abbé, was so severely wounded that he died on the following day, and two others were also injured. This produced a general combat. The citizens marched on the Seminary. The volunteers fired on everything, man or beast, which appeared in the streets, and it was not till the afternoon that the procureur of the Commune, with the assistance of some troops of the line, succeeded in restoring order. Scarcely, however, had he returned to the Hotel de Ville when the combat was renewed with still greater fury. The municipality persuaded Maillard to drive the volunteers into the Convent of St Francis. At five p.m. the Assembly was proclaimed by beat of drum, and martial law proclaimed. The procureur, carrying the red flag, and followed by a piquet of the grenadiers of the 42nd regiment, went round to all the posts of the volunteers and ordered them to retire. Maillard told Quenza that he held him responsible for all disorders. But Napoleon was unwilling to evacuate the Seminary and to retire to St Francis. He therefore got hold of the abbé Coti, who was Procureur Syndic of the district, and persuaded him to take their side, and to give the appearance of legality to the action of the volunteers. Quenza wrote to him in Italian "You must, my dear Coti, sign a requisition of the following purport:—'I require the commandants of the battalion of National Guards not to leave their quarters in the Seminary, nor the posts which they occupy, because there is a conspiracy against public liberty and against the Constitution.'" He added, "Prepare to come to us tonight; many *paesani* are arriving at this moment." And Napoleon added in French, without his signature, "The Corsicans have left for Corte— courage, courage."

Coti did what he was requested, although it was illegal. At 7.30 p.m. he ordered Maillard to give every assistance to the volunteers. Maillard replied at nine p.m. that the town demanded the retirement of the volunteers, and that he could not change the orders given by the legitimate authorities. Napoleon, unwilling to leave the Seminary, wrote to Maillard that some brigands were firing without respecting the flag of peace, that the same brigands were occupying all the exits of the Hotel de Ville, that the municipality could not deliberate freely, that the volunteers had obeyed the proclamation of the municipality, but that they were in the most imminent danger, and therefore he begged Maillard to leave them in their quarters, the only refuge which remained to them. He even paid a visit to Maillard in the citadel. He answered for the behaviour of the volunteers, but said that they could neither leave the Seminary nor take up their quarters in the Convent of St Francis. He promised that if the municipality would withdraw their requisition he would dismiss the *paesani*, who might cause annoyance to the inhabitants. But that very night Napoleon attempted to take by surprise the house of the Benielli, situated on the Colletta, the highest part of the city. He also occupied the houses which were close to the former college of the Jesuits, and thus had possession of a whole quarter of the town. The volunteers committed acts of pillage, seized the flour of the mills, devastated the country, and killed the cattle. This conduct cannot be defended.

On Easter Tuesday, 10 April, a conference was held at the citadel in the afternoon, between the municipality and Maillard on the one hand, and Quenza, Bonaparte, and three other officers of volunteers on the other, and at six p.m. a kind of armistice was drawn up. Quenza and Bonaparte promised to keep their men in good order, while the civil authorities ordered the citizens to commit no act of violence against the volunteers. Peace seemed to be established; but on the following morning Maillard wrote, "We are always in the greatest uncertainty, and our condition is very critical." The volunteers continued to kill the cattle, and to ravage the fields, to intercept provisions, and to prevent access to the fountains. The National Guards were reinforced by twelve hundred *paesani* from the neighbourhood. Napoleon visited the advanced posts on horseback, and said to the three hundred men who were quartered in the Capuchin Convent, that the whole nation had been outraged, in their person, but that justice would be done, and the guilty punished. Maillard reminded Quenza that according to the orders of Rossi, the volunteers ought to be broken up, but he received no answer.

The Directory of the district, who could not allow the soldiers and the citizens to die of hunger, sent three of its members at ten a.m. with a white flag, to visit the posts of the volunteers at the Capuchin Convent, the Genoese Tower, the new barracks, and the Seminary. The volunteers refused to listen to them, and some cried that they would agree to peace if the municipality would deliver up to them twelve sailors. Napoleon, apparently, hoped to corrupt the soldiers of the 42nd regiment. He told one of them that Maillard was an aristocrat. He said, "Your regiment comes from France, and you have sufficient experience of plots and revolutions to know who are the enemies of your country." He also took other steps with the assistance of Massaria, who has written an account of these events. However, their attempt was communicated to Maillard, and the soldiers swore to obey him and the municipality, and to defend the city of Ajaccio, to which they had always been attached, to the last extremity. Indeed, the communications of Massaria were received with indignation and contempt.

Meantime there was a deficiency of bread and wood in the town, no one could go out to work in the fields, the poor were in a piteous state, no one could go to the wells to draw water. The municipality determined to crush the resistance of Quenza and Bonaparte by force. A blank cartridge was to be fired, and if within an hour afterwards the battalion of volunteers had not left the Seminary and taken its position at the Convent of St Francis outside the town, the troops would fire with ball. Napoleon wrote to Maillard: "You wish to precipitate action, and everything will be ruined. Then the enemies of the Constitution will triumph, of whom there are only too many in this town. The destruction of the country, which we hope to avert, will be certain. Only reflect! These hasty measures ought to make you see that the municipality is not free—we protest against them."

This letter reached Maillard at seven p.m., just as the cannon of alarm was being fired. Two field-pieces were despatched, manned by the gunners of Napoleon's own regiment, the 4th, together with one hundred soldiers, and some sappers, and an officer of the municipality. But nothing was done; perhaps it was thought the 42nd regiment could not be trusted. At midnight a council of war was held in the citadel. At eight a.m. on 12 April, the guns were again brought out. Napoleon said, "So much the better; we shall cut the knot with the sword;" and he urged Quenza to advance against the guns, and to capture them. But he showed that nothing serious would be done. Indeed, on the same day two Commissioners, Cesari and Arrighi, were sent to Ajaccio by the Directory to restore peace. Napoleon, however, determined to end with a piece of audacity. He wrote to the municipality that Quenza had received from the Directory the authority to call together the National Guards of the interior, and from Paoli the positive order to maintain the posts of the Seminary, the new barracks, St Francis, and the Capuchins. He held the municipal body responsible for the destruction of the town. He said that if in an hour the guns had not disappeared, he would send messages into all the villages to come and put down the enemies of the Constitution by force, and that he had great difficulty in restraining his volunteers. The result was that a convention was concluded, and the cannons were withdrawn into the citadel.

Peace reigned once more, and the shops were opened. On 13 April, when the municipality was preparing to send the Mayor Levie, and the *juge de paix*, with Drago and two others, to meet the Commissioners, an officer of the volunteers went to the Hotel de Ville to say that no one would be permitted to leave the town, excepting the Mayor Levie. The municipality protested, and Levie refused to go without his colleagues, so that Bonaparte met the Commissioner alone at Bocognano, and gave him an account of what had occurred. On 14 April, Cervoni, the secretary of the Commissioners, made his appearance with Volney, and Volney required from Quenza, in the name of the municipality, a list of the volunteers, and of the posts which they occupied, and reminded Quenza that the volunteers ought, according to the convention, to destroy the fortifications of the houses which they had occupied. But Quenza did nothing; indeed, on 15 April, Volney was prevented from leaving the town. Arrighi and Cesari arrived on 16 April. They sent the *paesani* back to their villages, and ordered the battalion Quenza-Bonaparte to retire to Corte. Napoleon did his best to oppose this order, as being humiliating to the volunteers, but was persuaded by Joseph to yield.

The Commissioners, however, decided against the town, and arrested and imprisoned thirty-five citizens of Ajaccio. They also supported the action of Coti. On the whole they defended the conduct of the volunteers. How far their report was influenced by the suggestions of Napoleon cannot be known. The whole of this transaction, obscure as it is, and difficult to appreciate without taking into account the peculiarities of the Corsican character and the bitter quarrel which was then raging between the Church and the Constitution, is of the highest value for the appreciation of the character of Napoleon. We see him now, for the first time, as a man of action, of exceptional character and energy, ready to work and to brave all dangers. He is invigorated with the spirit of command. But under his boyish intemperance we can discern rare qualities of mind and character. He is never still; he is equally effective when he plans and when he fights, when he writes and when he talks, and during the whole of this confusion he is able to keep in check the motley masses of the volunteers and the national guard. He shows himself born for the conduct of great affairs.

The town of Ajaccio, however, was irritated with Napoleon; Peraldi and Pozzo di Borgo never forgave him. Pozzo said, "Napoleone Buonaparte è causa di tutto," and called him a "Corso Giurdan," a Jourdan of Corsica, referring, of course, to Jourdan coupe-tête, expressions inspired by Corsican hatred, and extremely unjust. Peraldi drew up a terrible indictment against the two brothers: "To take vengeance on the party opposed to them, they seize the opportunity of a private quarrel; they fire on innocent citizens, and do not listen to the voice of the law; they despise the orders of the municipality; they issue orders to neighbouring municipalities; they devastate property, blockade an entire city, renew the horrors of the reign of Charles IX; and finally conclude a treaty of peace as if they were a hostile power. This new St Bartholomew cannot remain unpunished."

Napoleon went to Corte, and on his way had an interview with Paoli. He proposed to resign his present post and to take command of a new battalion of volunteers which was to be raised by the Department. Paoli agreed, which shows that he had not formed a bad opinion of the youthful colonel, but on 13 May at Corte, he told Joseph that he could not carry out this design, because in future the bodies of volunteers would be separated, and not united under a single head. Napoleon had indeed determined to return to France. His position in his regiment was more than precarious. At the review, held on 1 January 1792, his name is thus recorded: "Buonaparte, first lieutenant, whose permission of absence has expired, is in Corsica." He was not one of those recommended to the National Assembly as having legitimate motives for absence. He was indeed regarded as an *emigré*, and we find opposite his name in a list of lieutenants, "Has given up his profession, and has been replaced on February 6th, 1792." It was high time that he went to Paris to place his fortunes once more on the road to success.

CHAPTER IX

PARIS

Napoleon reached Paris on 28 May 1792. The war, which he believed impossible, had been declared by the Legislative Assembly on 10 April, and the French had at first met with defeats. He wrote to Joseph on 29 May, "I arrived at Paris yesterday. I am, for the present, lodging at the same hotel as Pozzo di Borgo, Leonetti, and Peraldi, that is the Hotel des Patriotes Hollandais, Rue Royale. I find it too dear, and shall therefore change either today or tomorrow. I have only seen Pozzo di Borgo for a moment; our attitude was somewhat constrained, but at the same time friendly. Paris is in the most serious convulsions. It is flooded with strangers, and the discontented are very numerous. The National Guard, which remained at the Tuileries to guard the king, has been doubled. The bodyguard of the king will be dissolved, as they say that it was very badly composed. The news from the frontiers is always the same; it is probable that our troops will retire in order to carry on a defensive war. Desertion is very frequent amongst the officers. Our position is critical in every respect. Keep in close relations with General Paoli—he has all the power and is everything; he will be everything in the future, which, however, no one can foresee. I shall go to the Assembly today for the first time; it has not the same reputation as the Constituante."

On 14 June he writes again: that he has dined with M. Permon, and found Madame very amiable; that Servan, Roland, and Clavière have been dismissed, and that their places are taken by Dumouriez, Naillac, whom Napoleon knew well at Valence, and Morgues. He continues, "This country is riddled in all directions by the most bitter partisanship; it is difficult to discover the thread of so many different projects: I do not know how it will turn out, but everything tends to a revolution." He writes, on 18 June: "There are in France three parties, one in favour of the Constitution as it is, one against the Constitution, but in favour of liberty, the principles of which it supports. It desires a change, but a change within the limits of the Constitution; these two parties are united, and tend, for the moment, to the same end: the maintenance of the law, of tranquillity, and of all constituted authorities. They are all in favour of the war. The third party think the Constitution absurd, and would prefer a despot." It may be remarked that this description of French parties does not exhibit any great knowledge or insight. He continues, "We must contrive that Lucien shall remain with the General; it is most probable that all this will end by our becoming independent; act on this supposition."

Napoleon witnessed the disgraceful scenes of 20 June. Bourienne tells us that he had an engagement with Napoleon to dine with him at a restaurant in the Rue St Honoré near the Palais Royal, but that, seeing a body of five or six thousand men coming from the quarter of Les Halles, they followed them to the terrace, by the side of the river, to observe the movements of this disorderly crowd, who showed, by their words and their cries, that they belonged to the most abject of the people. Napoleon gave the following account of it to Joseph on 22 June: "The day before yesterday seven or eight thousand men, armed with pikes, axes, swords, muskets, spits, and pointed sticks, went to the Assembly to present a petition, and after that they went to the king. The garden of the Tuileries was closed, and was guarded by fifteen hundred National Guards. The mob threw down the gates, entered the palace, pointed cannon against the apartments of the king, broke open four doors, presented to the king two cockades—one white and the other tricolour—of which they gave him the choice. 'Choose,' they said, 'to reign here or at Coblentz.' The king behaved well: he put on the red, and the queen and the prince did the same. They gave the king something to drink. They remained four hours in the palace. All this is unconstitutional, and sets a very dangerous example; it is difficult to foresee what will become of the empire under these stormy circumstances."

Napoleon's principal object in coming to Paris had been to recover his place in the army, and we may assume that he took steps in this direction immediately on his arrival. On 21 June a departmental committee of the artillery sent a report to the effect that Napoleon had been actually deprived of his commission, but that he had explained the circumstances which had detained him in Corsica, and that they were completely satisfactory. They said that Peraldi had given contrary evidence, but that he was probably misinformed, and that they were of opinion that Napoleon should have the justice which he claimed. In consequence of this, the Minister of War wrote to Napoleon on 10 July, and informed him that he was to be replaced in the fourth regiment of artillery with the rank of captain. He also advised him to join his regiment. His commission, dated 6 February 1792, was signed by Servan on 30 August, and was, of course, in the name of the king. A facsimile of it is given by M. Masson. Napoleon also received his arrears of pay, amounting to more than £40. It is a curious fact that on 8 July, two days before the letter which gave Napoleon the commission of captain, the Minister of War wrote to Maillard in Corsica. "Having examined your report with the most serious attention, I am convinced that no one could have shown more prudence, moderation, and zeal for the public service, for the maintenance of good order, than you have done, in the disagreeable and very delicate circumstances in which you were placed, and that Messrs. Quenza and Bonaparte were infinitely reprehensible in the conduct which they held, and that one cannot disguise the fact that they favoured all the disorders and excesses of the regiment which they commanded." He adds, that if their offences were merely of a military character, he would bring them before a court-martial, but that according to existing laws they must be brought before civil tribunals. It is hardly conceivable that the same individual can have had complete acquaintance with these two letters; it is possible that, although bearing the same signature, they were issued from different departments. But Napoleon knew that the threat meant nothing. He wrote to Joseph, "The affair is finished; it has been sent from the War Office to the Ministry of Justice because there is no military offence; that is just what I wished."

In the same letter, dated 7 August, he also says, "I believe that I shall make up my mind to leave soon, and to surrender my commission in the volunteers, and that whatever turn events may take, I shall find myself established in France. If I had only consulted the interest of our house and my own inclination, I should have come to Corsica, but you all agree in this, that I ought to rejoin my regiment, therefore I shall do so." But the next three days brought a great change. The insurrection of 10 August had taken place, of which he gave the following account at St Helena. "At the sound of the tocsin and at the news that the Tuileries was being attacked, I ran to the Carrousel, to the house of Fauvelet, brother of Bourrienne, who had a furniture shop there. He had been my school-fellow at the military school of Brienne, and from that house I could watch without difficulty all the details of the day. Before I arrived at the Carrousel, I had been met in the Rue des Petits Champs, by a group of hideous men carrying a head on the end of a pike. Seeing me well dressed, and looking like a gentleman, they came to me to make me cry, 'Vive la Nation!' which I did without difficulty, as you may believe. The château was attacked by the violent mob. The king had for his defence, at least as many troops as the Convention had on Vendemiaire 13th, when they had to fight against a better-disciplined and more formidable enemy. The greater part of the national guard was on the side of the king—one must do them this justice. When the palace had been fired, and the king had taken refuge in the bosom of the Assembly, I ventured to penetrate into the garden. Never since have any of my battlefields given me such an idea of death as the mass of the Swiss corpses then presented to me, whether the smallness of the space made the number appear larger, or whether it was because I was to undergo this experience for the first time. I saw women respectably dressed committing the worst indecencies on the corpses of the Swiss. I visited all the *cafés* in the neighbourhood of the Assembly; everywhere the irritation was extreme, rage was in every heart, it showed itself in all faces, although the people present were not by any means of the lower class, and all these places must have been daily frequented by the same customers, for although I have nothing peculiar in my dress, but perhaps my countenance was more calm, it was easy to see that I excited many looks of hostility and defiance as being unknown and a suspect."

On the same day Napoleon wrote to his brother Joseph a full account of what had occurred, which he read to the members of the Directory, but the letter has since unfortunately disappeared. He said in it that if Louis XVI had shown himself on horseback, he would have gained the victory. Events occurred which compelled Napoleon to go to Corsica: a decree was passed on 17 August, by the Legislative Assembly, which ordered the confiscation and the sale of all religious houses. Marianna would be compelled to leave St Cyr, and there was no place for her to lodge in Paris. On 30 August Napoleon had an interview with Monge, and asked from him a commission as lieutenant-colonel of the Marine Artillery—an employment which would take him to Corsica. He was already lieutenant-colonel in the Corsican volunteers, and he was attached to the artillery; this appointment would combine the rank and the service. Monge, however, refused to grant his request.

The next day, 1 September, after passing on the road some bodies of volunteers who shouted, "Vive la Nation!" Napoleon went to the College of St Cyr. The directors refused to let Marianna depart without an order of the municipality, and another from the Directory of the district of Versailles. He then sought out the mayor of the village. He was a poor grocer named Aubrun, a very sensible man, who held the office for thirty-eight years. He lived in a dirty little shop just opposite the gate of the Cemetery of St Louis. Aubrun went with Napoleon to the College, and sent for Marianna. She told him that she would be in great difficulty if she undertook alone the long journey from St Cyr to Ajaccio. She begged to be allowed to have the escort of her brother, and Aubrun wrote down that he judged that it was necessary to give the permission. Napoleon then approached the Directory of the district of Versailles, his petition and that of his sister being written on the back of Aubrun's certificate. Marianna declared that she had never known any father but her brother, and that if he did not take her away, she could not leave the establishment. Napoleon said that he was obliged to leave Paris on important business, and he begged the officials to pay the expense of Marianna's journey. The Directory immediately voted the sum of 352 francs, and authorized Napoleon to remove his sister with her clothes and her linen. That very evening Napoleon came in a shabby cab and carried his sister off.

It is not certain, however, whether he left the capital immediately. Although he never admitted it, it is probable that he was in Paris during the massacre of September—indeed, it would have been difficult for him to have left until the barriers were open. It is likely that there would have been some delay in realizing Marianna's money. Napoleon most probably left Paris on 9 September, took boat at Lyons, stopped a short time at Valence, and then reached Marseilles. It is said that at Marseilles the mob, seeing that his sister wore feathers in her hat, surrounded the door of the hotel, and cried, "Death to the aristocrats!" Napoleon took off his sister's hat and threw it away among the crowd, with the words, "Not more aristocrats than you." Upon which the threats were turned into cheers.

Napoleon remained some time at Marseilles, partly from the difficulty of finding a ship and partly to receive the money due to him from Grenoble. He embarked, probably, on 10 October at Toulon, and arrived at Ajaccio on 15 October 1792.

When he reached his home he found that Joseph had not been successful in his candidature for the Convention. Madame Letizia had, for the first time since her husband's death, all her children gathered around her. Marianna, who had been called Elisa at St Cyr, that she might not be confused with Marianna de Casabianca, was received with joy, and was called "La Grande Demoiselle." She had excellent manners and considerable ability. Louis says of her that from the first day they became the best friends in the world. She was a thorough Bonaparte in character: proud, resolute, independent, active, and enterprising, able to hold her own against her brothers. When she became Grand Duchess of Tuscany she was her own Minister of Foreign Affairs, and exercised a sort of control over Pauline and Caroline. Joseph says of her that of the three sisters, she both morally and physically most resembled Napoleon. His brother Lucien writes of Napoleon at this time his belief that he would be a dangerous man under a free government, that he has a tendency to be a tyrant, and that he would prove one if he were ever king, and that his name would be a name of horror amongst posterity and in the mind of a sensitive patriot. Lucien's idea of tyranny, at this time, was affected by the principles of the Revolution, and experience has shown that Napoleon's name is regarded with horror, not so much by supporters of democratic governments as by statesmen of the type of Metternich. At the same time Lucien is indignant that his brother should have dissimulated his popular sympathies in talking with the ladies of St Cyr; he is in favour of a more decided and uncompromising course, and he is afraid that Napoleon will make sacrifices of principle for his advancement, and perhaps even change his opinions. Younger brothers do not always criticize their elder brothers with great indulgence, and these two statements may be left to contradict each other.

CHAPTER X

LA MADDALENA

Napoleon, on his arrival, resumed his position as second lieutenant-colonel of the volunteers. The battalion had six companies at Corte, while the three others were at Bonifacio under the command of Quenza. Napoleon went to Corte, and found his soldiers in an unsatisfactory state of discipline. But he did not wish to make a fuss about it. He wrote to Quenza, "Paoli is much discontented with the battalions, and especially with ours. We must not give ourselves away, which would be contrary to your policy. We must punish the officers and soldiers who resist discipline, but only in the last extremity." He then returned to Ajaccio. In the general uncertainty of his fortunes, he had some idea of going to India and serving in the English army against the natives, or possibly with the natives against the English. He added laughingly, that Uncle Fesch might accompany him as a missionary. Fesch would preach and baptize, and his nephew would occupy his spare time by lecturing on science and philosophy. However, he was soon engaged in an expedition against the island of Sardinia, in which his volunteers took part, although the events of it do not add much to his military reputation.

Sardinia at this time seemed inclined to throw off the yoke of its sovereign and to assume independence, and it was determined to dispatch an expedition to assist her. The government of France was now, during the suspension of the monarchy, in the hands of the Comité Exécutif provisoire, and they determined that the expedition should be commanded by Paoli. But the great man was now, with the title of general of division, at the head of the military power of Corsica, and his presence in the island was regarded as necessary, Anselme, therefore, who was at Nice, was appointed in his place. He was to embark at Marseilles on the fleet which was commanded by Admiral Truguet, taking with him the infantry of the army of the south and some volunteers from Marseilles; he was to collect at Bastia and Calvi such troops as these two towns could supply, and to land at Ajaccio, where he would be reinforced by three thousand regular troops and volunteers. Anselme and Truguet had full powers and were to act together, taking the advice of Paoli and Peraldi. Sémonville, who was proceeding as ambassador to Constantinople, was also to assist. He was very sanguine, and declared that the expedition would only leave the harbour of Sardinia to sail triumphantly into the Black Sea, and to arrest the ambition of Russia in the Crimea. The plan of Truguet was to seize Cagliari and the islands of La Maddalena as soon as possible, and to open a new granary for the departments of the south. The general opinion in Corsica was in favour of the enterprise, but the non-juring and Church party disapproved of it, because it might lead to the invasion of the States of the Church and the destruction of St Peter's. Anselme, however, refused to leave Nice, and his second in command, Brunet, did the same, so that the command was given to Raffaelle Casabianca, whom Napoleon afterwards qualified as a brave, simple man, but absolutely incapable.

Truguet arrived at Ajaccio, where he was to meet Casabianca. He became very intimate with the Bonaparte family, and danced with them nearly every evening, dancing being one of their favourite occupations. He fell in love with Elisa, who indeed preferred him to Baciocchi, whom she afterwards married. But neither of them brought the matter to a conclusion, and Truguet lamented at a later period that he had missed his fortune. Sémonville also stayed with the Bonapartes. He had with him his wife, widow of M. de Montholon, and her four children, two boys and two girls. Napoleon became much attached to Charles de Montholon, who afterwards accompanied him to St Helena, and gave him lessons in mathematics. Sémonville agreed to take Lucien with him as secretary. When Madame Letizia established herself in Paris, after the Italian campaigns of her son, the intimacy between the two families became still closer. Pauline lived with Madame Sémonville, and Louis and Jerome Bonaparte, as well as Eugène Beauharnais, entered the school of M. Lemaire, in which Charles de Montholon was already a pupil. The younger members of the two families treated each other as brothers and sisters.

The relations between the sailors and the Corsican volunteers were not very promising. They disembarked at Ajaccio in the first week of December, and threatened to hang the National Guards. On 18 December they hanged two volunteers, cut their bodies up, and carried the fragments about the streets, upon which the volunteers seized their arms and threatened to kill the sailors. It was obvious from this that the sailors and volunteers would never work together in harmony. Paoli, therefore, kept the volunteers at home, and gave Truguet the whole of the 42nd regiment, and drafts from the 26th and 52nd. Truguet's squadron set sail on 8 January 1793. Napoleon said, at a later period, that never was an enterprise conducted with less prudence or ability. But at the time he believed that he could succeed, and on 12 June he wrote to a friend that the fleet ought to get possession of Cagliari. There was no discipline either among the sailors or among the four thousand desperadoes who had been embarked at Marseilles. Napoleon said afterwards that they were anarchists, who carried terror everywhere, who were always looking only for aristocrats and priests, and were thirsting for blood and crime. As a matter of fact, after making a sort of attack on Cagliari on the night of 15 February, the Marseillais were seized with a panic, turned and ran away, throwing away their muskets, their haversacks, and even their clothes. They gained their ships, and departed with cries of "Treason!" and threats of hanging Casabianca on a lantern.

In order to assist the expedition against Cagliari, Truguet formed the plan of a naval attack on the north of Sardinia, to be carried out by the volunteers under Colonel Colonna Cesari Rocca. Cesari, who disapproved of the enterprise altogether, consented with reluctance. He took with him the corvette called *La Fauvette*, two hundred and fifty grenadiers of the 52nd regiment, and four hundred and fifty volunteers, the flower of the flock. He had on board ship provisions for six hundred combatants for forty or fifty days, and two large cannons. He set sail from Bonifacio on 18 February, Napoleon with him. Corsicans, who served as his secretaries at that period, have left a record that he was remarkably clean in his habits; that he dictated his orders with rapidity; that he was very fond of tabular statements, and carried out the smallest details in order, regularity, and exactness. Others have reported that he sought to be informed about everything; that he was very neat in his attire; that he was most careful in dressing himself, washing himself every morning with a wet sponge, and having a dressing-case with fittings of silver marked with his initials.

The islands formerly called Buccinari, now Le Bocche, are situated in the Straits of Bonifacio, between Corsica and Sardinia. They were at this time inhabited by shepherds, labourers, and sailors, who were Corsican in language and customs, and lived a simple, hard-working life. The islands are eleven in number, the largest of them being Maddalena, which is guarded by two forts. Close to this is Caprera, which was the residence of Garibaldi at the close of his life. France claimed these islands on the ground of their having belonged to Genoa.

Cesari left Bonifacio, as we have before said, on the night of 18 February 1792, and the next day was in sight of the islands. But the fleet was detained by a calm, and was driven back to harbour by a strong wind. On 22 February, at nine a.m., Cesari started anew, but the volunteers refused to follow him, being afraid of sea-sickness and of the Sardinian galleys. Cesari, disregarding the volunteers, sailed to Maddalena, and they were shamed into following him. They anchored at the south-west of Maddalena, at the entrance of the canal which separates that island from San Stefano. At four p.m., protected by the fire of the *Fauvette*, the troops landed on San Stefano. The Sardinians met them on the rocks, and then retired to a large square tower at the extremity of Villa Marina. The Corsicans occupied San Stefano, and surrounded the tower. Napoleon was of opinion that they should have immediately constructed a battery against Maddalena, and carried that island by storm in the disturbance. By not doing this, the favourable moment was lost. On the following day the tower, garrisoned by twenty-five Swiss, was taken.

On the night of 23 February, Napoleon, who commanded both the artillery and the volunteers, built a battery, armed with a mortar and two small guns, opposite Maddalena and its two little forts. In his report to the Minister of War he declared that he fired upon the village both shells and red-hot shot; that he set it on fire four successive times; that he destroyed more than eighty houses, burnt a magazine of wood, and reduced the two forts to silence. The weather was terrible, with heavy rain and a strong wind. The cold was intense, and there was little or no wood, and scarcely any food, while the island contained five hundred combatants, soldiers, the militia of Gallura, and the inhabitants capable of bearing arms. Notwithstanding these obstacles, Napoleon hoped to be master of Maddalena on the following day. On the evening of 24 February Cesari determined to attack on the next morning at dawn. But the crew of the *Fauvette* were afraid. They saw the coast of Sardinia occupied with men and horses, and greatly exaggerated their number. They determined to set sail, and made their preparations accordingly. Cesari went on board the ship and did his best to recall them to duty. "Citizens," he cried, "why do you mutiny? What madness induces you to be faithless to your country and to yourselves?" They replied with one voice, "We will not stay." But immediate departure would have meant the sacrifice of the volunteers and the regular troops. Cesari said that if they did not obey, he would blow up the ship. Quenza and Bonaparte, to their great indignation, were compelled to retreat just as victory seemed certain.

The retreat took place in the greatest disorder; in fact, the second company of the grenadiers of the 52nd was nearly left behind. Napoleon, on 28 February, signed a paper which recognized the zeal and patriotism of

Cesari; but on 2 March he wrote to the Minister of War that the Corsican volunteers had been in need of every kind of munition—of tents, clothes, great-coats, of a train of artillery—but that their courage had supplied every defect, and that they would have succeeded if it had not been for their infamous abandonment by the corvette, and that the punishment of the cowards and the traitors, which caused the failure of the enterprise, was necessary to the interest and glory of the republic. The tension between the volunteers and the sailors is shown by an assault which was made on Napoleon in the public square of Bonifacio by some of the crew of the *Fauvette*.

The volunteers of Bocognano came to the rescue and saved their colonel, and would have killed the sailors if Napoleon had not prevented them from doing so. Whatever may be our judgment on the Maddalena expedition, its conduct casts no reflection on the character or the career of Napoleon.

CHAPTER XI

PAOLI

We now come to the history of the quarrel between Napoleon and Paoli, which was one of the most important events of his early manhood. We have seen that at this time Corsica was in a most disturbed condition, and that the relations between the French and the islanders were strained almost to breaking. In June 1791, the Assembly sent two Commissioners, Monestier and the Abbé Andrei, to Corsica, to inquire into the condition of affairs, and on their arrival they were met by strong complaints against the conduct of the Directory of the Department. It was natural that the Directory should not regard the Commissioners with favour; they could not deny their power, but they did their best to render their actions inoperative. Monestier reported that the island was in a state of anarchy, elections were a matter of intrigue or private enmity and friendship, justice did not exist, the election of the *juges de paix* was the cause of such domestic quarrels that they received the name of *juges de guerre*; more than a hundred and thirty homicides had taken place in three years, and only one person had been condemned for them. Agriculture was at a stand-still, the peasant could not work in the fields without a musket by his side, the roads were becoming useless, the forests were being laid waste. The public revenues were an object of public pillage, and large sums which had been given by the Minister of the Interior for draining the marshes of St Florent and Aleria went into private pockets, and no accounts were published. The Directory laid its hands upon all the revenues; it received the customs, now reduced by one-half, and used them in paying their officers, their relations, and their friends. The four battalions of National Guards cost about £2500 a month; this sum was regularly paid, but there were not more than twenty or twenty-five men in a company. The captains enriched themselves, and the finances of the volunteers were also in great disorder. Assignats were not received by tradesmen as payment in the island; they were discharged at Toulon or Marseilles for money which disappeared before it reached the hands of those entitled to it. Pillage was the order of the day.

Since 1790 there had been two Directories of the Department, one under the influence of Arena, the other of Saliceti; Pozzo di Borgo belonged to the first, and Joseph Bonaparte to the second. They were, however, characterized by the same faults and the same plunderings, and the same abuse of power. They were composed chiefly of young men, entirely without experience. Paoli was president of the Council General, but he took no part in the administration; he gave advice when he was asked for it, but did not interfere otherwise. On 11 September 1792, after the fall of the monarchy and the retirement of Rossi, Paoli was nominated by the Conseil Éxecutif Provisoire at Paris Lieutenant-General and Commandant of the 23rd division. He therefore concentrated in his hands both civil and military power, and no one doubted of his attachment to France. At the elections for the Convention, the conflict between Paoli and the Directory became apparent. The *babbo*, as he was called, wished the six members to be Saliceti, Cesari, Massaria, Andrei, Bozio, and Panattieri, and Paoli was to preside at the election. But he was laid up with fever, and Saliceti took his place. Saliceti secured the election of himself, Casabianca, Chiappe, and Moltedo, who were members of the Directory, Andrei and Bozio, so that three of the most important Paolists were excluded. Paoli recovered and determined to take his revenge. By a decree of the Convention, passed on 22 September, all municipal bodies had to be renewed, and not a single member of the Directory was re-elected. Paoli won a complete triumph, and the Council-General was composed exclusively of his adherents. At this time, Pozzo di Borgo, who had been a member of the Legislative, became Paoli's principal adviser. He was a well-educated lawyer with good manners, and Lady Elliot speaks of him as the only Corsican who was really distinguished. The *babbo* fell more and more under his influence, and Pozzo said of himself, "He is the head, I am the hand."

The chief adversary of Paoli was Saliceti, who, after playing a prominent part in the Revolution and under the Directory, became Minister of Police at Naples, under Murat. He died prematurely, and Napoleon, on hearing of his death, wrote to Murat, "You do not know what you have lost, and of what assistance this man might have been in a difficult time. He was one of those who always succeed." His character was unscrupulous, he loved money beyond everything, he was amiable and affectionate in private life, but cold and petulant in public affairs. There is a story that when he was once walking with Napoleon on a narrow ledge on the Riviera of Genoa,

A view of Ajaccio as it was at the time of Napoleon's birth.

An early photograph of Ajaccio.

Top left and right: Carlo Maria Buonaparte, (1746-1785). Buonaparte was a Corsican lawyer and politician who briefly served as a personal assistant to Pasquale Paoli and eventually became Corsica's representative to the court of Louis XVI.

Bottom left and right: Nobile Marie-Lætitia Buonaparte, née Ramolino, (1750-1836); wife to Carlo above; Madame Mère de l'Empereur; the mother of Napoleon.

The Bonaparte family house in Ajaccio. The top picture from an old drawing, the bottom photograph dating from the late nineteenth century.

Two old photographs of the room where Napoleon is reported to have been born.

An olive press on the ground floor of the Bonaparte home.

Entry for the baptism of Napoleon in the Ajaccio register for 1771. His baptism was some considerable time after his birth in 1769.

An anonymous portrait
of Napoleon as a child,
painted from memory.

A caricature drawn at
Brienne of Napoleon
and some schoolfellows.

A sketch drawn at
Brienne. Napoleon
prepared to defend
Paoli restrained by a
teacher; caricature by
a schoolfellow.

Napoleon aged 16.

The snowball fight at Brienne, Napoleon commanding the redoubt.

A sample of Napoleon's handwriting at the age of 16. Thoughts on suicide; (see appendix 1B).

An exercise undertaken by Napoleon, aged 19, at the Military College.

Napoleon as a lieutenant in the artillery.

Above left and Right: Filippo Antonio Pasquale di Paoli, (1725-1807). Following the French conquest of Corsica in 1768, Paoli oversaw the Corsican resistance. When the Corsican forces were defeated at Ponte Novu he was forced into exile in England. He returned after the French Revolution, but later broke with the revolutionaries and helped to create the Anglo-Corsican Kingdom which lasted between 1794 and 1796. After the island was re-occupied by France he again went into exile in London where he died in 1807.

Left: Antoine Christophe Saliceti, (1757-1809). Saliceti was born in Corsica. As deputy to the National Convention, Saliceti was sent home to Corsica on a mission to oversee Paoli and enforce the Reign of Terror; however, he was compelled to withdraw to Provence, where he took part in repressing the revolts at Marseille and Toulon. During this time he met and promoted his compatriot Napoleon.

Top left: Joseph-Napoleon Bonaparte, (1768-1844). Joseph was the elder brother of Napoleon, who made him King of Naples and Sicily (1806-1808), and later King of Spain (1808-1813, as José I.
Top right: Lucien Bonaparte, (1775-1840); Prince Français; 1st Prince of Canino and Musignano. Lucien held genuinely revolutionary views, which led to an often abrasive relationship with his brother Napoleon.

Bottom left: Louis Napoléon Bonaparte, (1778-1846); Prince Français; Comte de Saint-Leu, King of Holland (1806-1810). Louis had differences with his brother and as a result Napoleon took his Dutch kingdom away from him.
Bottom right: Jérôme-Napoléon Bonaparte, (1784-1860). In 1803, Jérôme married Elizabeth Patterson in the USA. This angered Napoleon, but he was unable to convince Pope Pius VII to annul their marriage, and therefore annulled it himself. He later married HRH Princess Catharina of Württemberg, (pictured here).

Top left: Maria Anna Elisa Bonaparte Baciocchi Levoy, (1777-1820); Princesse Française, Duchess of Lucca and Princess of Piombino, Grand Duchess of Tuscany, Countess of Compignano. Elisa married Felice Pasquale Baciocchi Levoy, a member of Corsican nobility.
Top right: Pauline Bonaparte, 1780-1825. Pauline was the first sovereign Duchess of Guastalla, an imperial French Princess and the Princess consort of Sulmona and Rossano. Pauline was Napoleon's favourite sibling.

Left: Maria Annunziata Carolina Murat, née Bonaparte, (1782-1839); Princesse Française, Grand Duchess Consort of Berg and Cleves, Queen Consort of Naples and Sicily, Princess Consort Murat.

A representation of Napoleon
on the Bridge of Arcola,
15-17 November 1796.

Napoleon at Milan, 1797.

This remarkable painting is by Jean Baptiste Greuze, (1725-1805); and depicts
Napoleon as First Consul, c. 1800, but looking deceptively boyish.

Le Souper de Beaucaire, Napoleon's 1793 political pamphlet, was completed on 29 July 1793, while he was a captain. He wrote it as a plea to end a civil war that was raging in the south of France during that summer. This painting is a much later representation of the fictional supper by Jean Lecomte du Nouÿ.

Batterie des Sans-Culottes, laid by Napoleon, Toulon, 1793; from a contemporary drawing.

Bulletin des Batteries
du 16 au 17 frimaire

Batterie de	
la Convention	L'ennemi a Tiré Vivement toute la nuit Contre Cette Batterie
des Obusiers	Cette Batterie n'est pas achevée par le Défaut de Travailleurs
farinière	L'on fait les Platter formes
Poudrière	L'ennemi a beaucoup Tiré Ce matin
Petite Rade	Rien de Nouveau
Montagne	Rien de Nouveau
Sans Culottes	les Vaisseaux Sont hors de la Portée
4 moulin	Quelques Coups de Canons Contre la Redoute angloise
Sans Peur	L'ennemi a Tiré beaucoup d'obusier nous avons eu un homme de Tué
Jacobine	une Obuse des ennemis nous a démonté une Pièce nous avons eu deux hommes de Tué
l'ablette	Quelques Coups de Canons Contre la Redoute angloise
fort Bregaillon	L'ennemi Construit une nouvelle Batterie au dela de L'Estme nous avons jetté Plusieurs bombes et Tiré Plusieurs Coups sur les Travailleurs
grande Rade	les Vaisseaux Sont hors de la Portée

Le commandant en second de l'artillerie

Buonaparte

Napoleon's official report on the batteries before Toulon, 7 December 1793.

the idea occurred to him of throwing the future Emperor into the sea. "We were alone," he relates, "and ten times did the idea occur to me to throw him into the sea; one blow and the world was changed." It is difficult to say which is most strange, that he should have conceived this idea, or that he should have avowed it. Napoleon as Emperor made use of Saliceti, but never allowed him near his person.

Saliceti had been a member of the Constituent Assembly, he was the leader of the Corsican patriots, and obtained the return of Paoli to the island, as he then respected and admired him. Paoli said that he loved him as a son, and he secured his election as Procureur Syndic of the department. Indeed, after Paoli, he was the most popular man in Corsica, and was regarded as a second Paoli, and as the second founder of the prosperity of his country. He was a warm supporter of the union with France. He said that if Corsica were isolated and independent it would be torn by factions and subject to foreign invasions, it would not be able to meet the expense of an army, a fleet, and an administration, it would be ruined by the smallest war, and was exposed to the attacks of Tunis, Algiers, and Genoa. It was much better to be united to France and to share in its prestige; to be associated with an empire the size of which would give consistency to the island, with a nation which could protect the Corsican coast, and secure its commerce. As for the volunteers, what would be more profitable than that two thousand Corsicans should receive their pay from France?

Gradually, however, the relations between Paoli and Saliceti became less friendly. Paoli thought that his conduct as Procureur Syndic was too arbitrary, and Saliceti became jealous of the *babbo*. He was also afraid lest some of his malversations should be discovered, and Pozzo threatened to inquire into them. He said, "When all the facts are known the people will open their eyes to the real merit of certain pretended eagles of genius, and their affectation of disinterested motives." In fact the new *régime* was not at all to Saliceti's taste. As member of the Convention, he wrote to Napoleon from Paris, that he regarded the last election as a counter-revolution, but that he was not afraid, and that misfortune was good, that the results would be happy for the country, and that in three or four months the cloud which covered the horizon would be dispersed.

Another adversary of Paoli was Bartolommeo Arena. He had begun by daubing Paoli with the coarsest flattery. He proposed to erect a statue of him, and when Paoli objected that his career was by no means terminated, Arena declared that the glory of the *babbo* was eternal. He held several appointments and was elected to the Legislative Assembly in Paris. Paoli despised him, and suspected him of malversation. An obscure Corsican quarrel with the rival family of Savelli turned love into hatred, and Arena became the mortal enemy of Paoli. He opposed him in every way, and denounced him as traitor to the Minister of War and to the Jacobins of Paris. He accused him of being more like a Pasha than a constitutional general, said that he was surrounded by a bodyguard, and that he had designs on the sovereignty of Corsica. In this quarrel he was amply supported by his brothers, Filippo Antonio and Giuseppe. Another member of the Arena-Saliceti party, the *"fazione Arena-Salicetariia"* as Pozzo calls it, was Gentili, who had been the secretary, the confidant, and the intimate friend of Paoli during his exile, but who now, for some obscure reason, broke with him. Volney also, who had left the island in disgust, and had gone to Paris, vented his disappointment on Paoli as he did upon the rest of the world.

Napoleon also determined to leave the side of Paoli, and to attach himself to that of Saliceti. He had some years before a great admiration for Saliceti, which is shown both in his letter to Buttafuoco and in his Lyons essay. In the beginning of 1793 Saliceti opened up a correspondence with Napoleon, in which he said, "I desire, my dear friend, that you would furnish me with an opportunity of showing how much I have at heart to give you a mark of friendship. You can count upon me entirely, and perhaps I shall not be altogether useless to you. Adieu! I embrace you, with your brother and all your family."

Napoleon became gradually more convinced that Corsica could never be independent, and his sympathies turned more and more to the side of France. He forgave the confiscation by the provincial Government of his estate at Milelli and the Boldrini mansion. He rejoiced in French victories. He said to Sémonville, after the execution of Louis XVI, "I have reflected much on our situation; the Convention has, without doubt, committed a great crime, and I deplore it more than anyone; but, whatever happens, Corsica must always be joined to France, and it can only exist on this condition; the cause of union will always be defended by me and mine." Paoli apparently made no effort to retain Napoleon. He is reported to have said to him once, "Napoleon, you have nothing modern about you, and you do not belong to this age; your feelings are those of a hero of Plutarch. Courage! You will take your flight." But a coolness grew up between them. Perhaps Paoli remembered the treacherous conduct of Charles Bonaparte, the father. He thought that the Bonapartes were restless, aggressive, and devoured by ambition, as undoubtedly they were. He refused to take Lucien as his secretary. He disapproved of the conduct of Joseph in the Directory; he passed Napoleon over for the post of *aide-*

de-camp. He is reported to have said to Sémonville, "Do you see that little man? He has in him two Mariuses and a Sulla." This irritation was kept up by the influence of Pozzo de Borgo, who regarded the Bonapartes as his mortal enemies. It is difficult for an Englishman to appreciate the strength of a Corsican vendetta.

In the Convention Saliceti was the only Corsican deputy, who voted for the death of Louis. The Provisional Government complained to him that Corsica contributed little to the common defence, that they did not pay their taxes, nor send their volunteers to the mainland, and that the island was in a state of anarchy. Saliceti admitted these charges and laid the blame on Paoli, who, he said, was influenced by men of perfidious intentions. War was declared against England on 1 February 1793. This tended to make Paoli unpopular, because he had lived twenty years in London, and had received a pension from George III. The result was that Paoli was summoned to Toulon. But he refused to go, alleging as reasons, his age and infirmities, the fear of sea-sickness, and the danger of leaving the country. A second summons to Nice was not more effectual. On 28 January and on 5 February 1793, Saliceti made speeches in the Convention about Corsica, which were not favourable to Paoli. Eventually Saliceti, with two other deputies, were sent to Corsica as Commissioners of the Convention. We need not pursue in detail the course of their intrigues, into which quite as much personal jealousy and hatred entered as zeal for the efficiency of the public service. Saliceti and his colleagues arrived at Bastia on 6 April 1793. A quarrel rose between the Commissioners and the Directory. On 13 April Saliceti had an interview with Paoli at Corte. He apparently persuaded the *babbo* to come to Bastia to confer with the Commissioners, and also advised him to retire from political life and go to Paris. The result of this was that, on 16 April, the three Commissioners sent a letter to Paoli begging him to come to Bastia to assist them in the work of reconciliation and peace. But on the following day the astonishing news arrived that the Convention had ordered the arrest of Paoli and Pozzo.

The cause of this *coup d'état* was Lucien, the brother of Napoleon, then a lad of eighteen. He had sublime confidence in himself, and cared little for the advice of his brothers. He had been Paoli's secretary for six months, and he has described with a fluent and romantic pen the old convent in which the general lodged, the noble simplicity of his life, the frugality of his meals, the magnificent forest of chestnuts which surrounded his abode, the goats guarded by shepherds lying in the shade of trees, and singing from hill to hill in answer to each other, like the shepherds of Theocritus and Vergil. He then describes how he returns to his home, he finds his mother writing at the side of Elisa, Pauline and Jerome playing together, Louis daubing with paints, Napoleon, in his uniform of lieut.-colonel, sitting at a window with Caroline on his knee playing with his watch-chain. The children are dismissed. Lucien says that Paoli is turning traitor, and has said, "Woe to those who take the side of the brigands, I will recognize none of them, not even the sons of Charles." At these words, Letizia, Joseph, and Napoleon pace up and down the room. Napoleon cries, "It is too much. Ah! Master Pascal declares war upon us; good, we will make war also." They decided to resist Paoli, and to defend Ajaccio against the mountaineers. Lucien says that he has given his word of honour to return, and that he must rejoin Paoli, whom he cannot leave. But his mother and Joseph command him to stay, and with tears he signs a letter written by Letizia and his two elder brothers. He says in it that he yields to the wishes of his family, but that he will always preserve the memory of Paoli. He gives this letter to the mountaineer, Lucchesi, to carry to Paoli, and bids him secretly to kiss the hand of the general.

All this is romance. Some days before this, Lucien had left Paoli on his own account because Sémonville had promised to take him as his secretary to Constantinople. Lucien followed his chief to France, and there solemnly denounced Paoli before the Republican Club of Toulon. From his memoirs it appears that this denunciation was unpremeditated, and that, called upon to speak upon the condition of Corsica, he was led by the general enthusiasm and applause to say what he did not intend, no unusual error for a young man to make. He said that Paoli was the tyrant and not the defender of his people, that he paid with French gold a Swiss regiment which was devoted to him, that he wished to be King of Corsica, that he exercised all the despotism of a sovereign, holding the island in degrading servitude, committing barbarous and arbitrary acts, neglecting the employment of juries, throwing citizens into prison and entombing his wretched victims in his Bastille at Corte. There was only one remedy—to dismiss Paoli immediately and to deliver him to the sword of the law. This denunciation was received by the Club with enthusiasm, and an address to the Convention was based upon it. It was presented to the Convention, on 2 April 1793, by Escudier, deputy for the Var. In his speech he accused Paoli of tyranny and treason, laid at his door the failure of the expedition to Sardinia, reproached him for his connection with England, and proposed to summon him to the bar, together with Pozzo di Borgo. Andrei begged the Convention to await the report of their Commissioners, but Escudier was supported by La Source, Marat, Cambon and Barère, who said that Paoli had become British, and that Pitt coveted the island. On the motion of Cambon, the Commissioners were ordered to get possession of Paoli and Pozzo by every means in their power. Lucien was very proud of his exploit, and wrote to his brothers that he had dealt a fatal blow to their enemies, which they had not anticipated. His letter was intercepted and brought to Paoli, who remarked, "What a little blackguard—he is capable of anything!" He published the letter, saying that he kept the original in order to devote the name of its writer to perpetual infamy.

On receiving the decree of the Convention, Saliceti was in despair, but he was obliged to execute it. He ordered Raffaelle Casabianca to take command of the 23rd division, and the municipality of Corte to arrest Paoli and Pozzo di Borgo. This was more easily said than done. The Corsicans were indignant; they flocked to Corte to prevent the arrest of their hero. The Directory endeavoured to support him; they printed in Italian the discussion in the Convention on 2 April, and the speech of Lucien at Toulon, adding a refutation. They then proceeded to rouse the country, and a civil war broke out. The Commissioners, with some difficulty, were able to hold Calvi, and they were sure of Saint Florent, and Bastia, but Bonifacio and Ajaccio escaped them. At Bonifacio, Quenza refused to acknowledge Casabianca, and declared that he remained faithful to Paoli, seized the military camp, and took possession of the magazine of arms and munitions of war.

What part were the Bonaparte family to play in this juncture? Joseph went to Saliceti and represented to him that the decree of 7 April, ordering the arrest of Paoli and Pozzo di Borgo, was worthy of the majesty of the Republic, which should be consistently on her guard, but that it was precipitate and forced the hand of the Commissioners. Napoleon was of the same opinion; he wrote to Quenza that he hoped that his battalion would not be suppressed. He believed that matters would be arranged and that the Commissioners would come to terms with Paoli. He was greatly disturbed at the decree, which took him by surprise. He saw that there would be a civil war, and that Paoli would certainly win at first, and would certainly not spare the Bonapartes. He therefore wrote a letter to the Convention begging them to withdraw the decree. He said that the Convention had passed laws each of which was a blessing. But the decree which summoned to its bar the aged and infirm Paoli had saddened the whole of Ajaccio. Paoli a conspirator! Why should he conspire?

To avenge himself on the Bourbons! They had exiled him, but his resentment, if he had any, must have been satisfied by the death of Louis. To restore the nobles and the priests? He had always fought against them. To deliver Corsica to the English? What would he gain by living in the slums of London? Was he then ambitious? What had he to desire? He was the patriarch of liberty, and the precursor of the French Republic; the Corsicans loved him and gave him their entire confidence; they gave him everything because they owed him everything, even the happiness of being Frenchmen and Republicans.

"Put calumny to silence," he concluded, "and the pernicious men who use it; recall your decree of April 2nd; give back joy to all this people and listen to their cry of sorrow." Besides this, he drew up a petition to the municipality of Ajaccio, in which he suggested that they should convoke a meeting in which all the citizens should swear that they would die French Republicans.

But the Bonapartes had lost their influence in the town. The events of Easter, 1792, were not forgotten. The new mayor, Guitera, was an ardent Paolist. The Patriotic Club, which supported Saliceti, was met by a new club, called the Society of the Incorruptible Friends of the People, the Law, Liberty, and Equality, founded by Mario Peraldi. This club declared itself ardently on the side of Paoli. Attempts made by Napoleon to reconcile the two parties, and to come to an understanding with Paoli, proved ineffectual. On 26 April Paoli addressed to the Convention a dignified and moderate letter, regretting that his age and infirmities prevented him from coming to them in person, and confounding his accusers, declaring his devotion to France, and his willingness to retire from Corsica if his presence there was a cause of distrust or hatred. The Convention, the Executive Council, and the Committee of Public Safety, fearing to drive the Corsicans to despair, determined to recall the decree of 2 April. The letter of Paoli was read before the Assembly on 16 May, and the Committee wrote to the Commissioners counselling a careful and a moderate action. A week later Barère announced that two fresh Commissioners would be sent to Corsica to arrange matters; they were Antiboul and Bo, and on 5 June, again on the proposition of Barère, the Convention determined to suspend the decree of 2 April until the report of Antiboul and Bo should have been received.

This was the epoch of the fall of the Girondists, which caused disturbances throughout the whole of France. Antiboul and Bo were arrested in Marseilles by the revolted sections, and Paoli, who supported the Girondists, was confirmed in his rebellion. He endeavoured to separate two of the Commissioners, Delcher and Lacombe Saint Michel, from Saliceti, but he found that all three were warmly attached to each other. He then suggested that they had come to the island with the purpose of making an arrangement with Genoa for surrendering Corsica in exchange for the Gulf of Spezzia, Volney having persuaded the French to get rid of so costly a possession. The opposition to the Commissioners broke out into open rebellion, and the rebels expected assistance from England or Spain. The peasants traversed the country crying, "Evviva il Generale Paoli!" and the houses of those who were not favourable to the *babbo* were attacked. The Commissioners, on their side, began to employ force. They created a new Directory, and changed the capital from Corte to Bastia; they cashiered Quenza, and publicly condemned Paoli. The civil war in Corsica was an echo of that which was raging in many parts of France between the partisans of the Mountain and those of the Gironde.

At the end of April Napoleon was still in Ajaccio, and was doing his best to recover that city for the Convention. He tried to get possession of the citadel, and even thought of bombarding it. Paoli wrote on 5 May: "Napoleon Bonaparte, Abbatucci, and I believe Meuron, and some others of their friends, have endeavoured during these last days to drive the National Guard from the citadel of Ajaccio, as if the fortresses were more secure for the Republic in the hands of troops of the line than in the hands of Corsican volunteers."

At this time the action of Lucien Bonaparte in inducing the club at Toulon to approach the Convention became known, and that Joseph was with the Commissioners at Bastia, and was a confidant of Saliceti. Thus the opinion prevailed both at Corte and Ajaccio that the decree against Paoli and Pozzo had been contrived by the Saliceti party, of which the Bonapartes were prominent members. Napoleon, therefore, determined to leave Ajaccio, and to join the Commissioners at Bastia.

The adventures he went through form a most romantic story. He left the town on foot with one of his own peasants, Nicola Frate, of Bocognano, to whose son he left 10,000 francs in his will. He soon became aware that if he continued his journey he would be arrested, so he determined to return to Ajaccio and to endeavour to reach Bastia by sea. At Bocognano he was stopped by some peasants, stirred up by Mario Peraldi, and confined in a room on the ground floor of a house which looked in the street. At night he escaped out of the window, and accompanied by two friends, Felice Tusoli and Marcaggi, both of whom he richly rewarded, went to Ucciani, where the mayor, Poggioli, whom he also mentioned in his will, gave him assistance. It was now daylight, and he did not dare to re-enter the town, so he concealed himself in the grotto of a garden belonging to his uncle, Nicola Paravicini, and at nightfall went to the house of his cousin, John Jerome Levie, who had been mayor in the previous year. He then went to bed and slept peacefully. The next night he also slept well, and the following day he spent in reading Rollin's history. But towards evening Levie became aware that the retreat of the fugitive was discovered, and that the Grenadiers were out in search of him. Napoleon was just about to proceed to the shore, where he would find a boat, when a loud knock was heard at the door. Levie sent his cousin into his room, and the rest of the garrison—for the house had been placed in a state of defence—into another apartment. The brigadier of the gendarmes entered alone. He said, "I am looking for Napoleon Bonaparte, and have been ordered to search your house." Levie replied that he was much offended, that he was a peaceable citizen, and that he had been mayor of the town, and that the gendarmes might search his house from top to bottom, but that they would find nothing. The brigadier replied, with an appearance of relief, that he was satisfied with Levie's word; he drank a glass of wine, and retired, after making his apologies.

Napoleon took leave of Madame Levie with perfect calmness, came down the staircase opening through the cellar, the garden and the stables, and reached the shore. There a French boat took them to the ship. The sailors, who were waiting with impatience, received him gladly, and Levie took his leave. Napoleon went by sea to Macinaggio, and thence by way of Rogliano to Bastia, hiding in a wretched house which he had hired with difficulty. Napoleon, in his will, left 100,000 francs to Levie, his widow, his children, and his grand-children.

Napoleon advised the Commissioners to concentrate all their efforts on St Florent, to fortify it strongly, and to entrench themselves there until they received assistance from France. He also urged them to gain possession of Ajaccio, saying that the town was on their side, with the exception of those who were under the influence of Peraldi. On 23 May, Lacombe Saint Michel, Saliceti, Napoleon, and Joseph left the bay of St Florent in the middle of the night. They took with them four hundred regular troops, some gunners, and a few gendarmes. The artillery, under the orders of Napoleon, consisted of two mortars and some cannon, embarked on the corvette *La Belette*, the brig *Le Hasard*, and some other smaller vessels. After being seven days at sea in bad weather, they arrived in the harbour of Ajaccio, where they saw the standard of the Republic hoisted on the citadel. They anchored on the opposite side of the harbour, close to the old tower of Campitello. The troops disembarked on 1 June, but they were only joined by twenty-three Swiss of the Regiment Salis-Grisons and six soldiers of the 52nd, together with some citizens, amongst whom was the Abbé Coti, Procureur Syndic of the district, a friend of the Bonapartes. The Commissioners sent an imperious message to the municipality ordering them to surrender. But they replied that the town was attached to the French Republic, but that they would not receive the Commissioners, while the soldiers and sailors sent them a message begging them to retire, saying that the Corsicans and French Republicans would submit to the law of the Convention, but that they rejected the presence and the partiality of Saliceti. The troops remained during the day of 2 June at Campitello and re-embarked in the morning. Coti informed them that they could expect no assistance, as Colonna-Leca, who commanded the citadel, had disarmed the greater part of the inhabitants, and had trained his guns on the houses of the patriots. In fact, the Paolists were receiving reinforcements every moment, and the National Guards of the neighbouring parishes were coming to their support. The whole affair had ended in nothing.

Civil war had indeed broken out. Calvi was attacked by Leonetti, who called out to the troops which garrisoned it that they should pay dearly for the blood of their king. On 16 May 1793 the Council General, which was faithful to Paoli, summoned a Corsican parliament to meet at Corte. They met to the number of a thousand, on 21 May, in the Convent of St Francis. More than two thousand Corsicans awaited their decision in the public square. Paoli and Pozzo, being sent for, entered the hall of deliberation amidst the firing of guns and the applause of the people of the Congress. Paoli affirmed his unshakable attachment to the Republic. The meeting proclaimed him as father of his country, and condemned the decree of 2 April. Those who refused to acknowledge the authority of Saliceti, Delcher and Lacombe Saint Michel, Paoli and Pozzo were to be retained in their offices, and Saliceti, Moltedo, and Casabianca were deprived of their positions as representatives because they had outraged their duty and lost all confidence. On 29 May, in the last meeting of the Parliament, a violent resolution was passed against the families of Arena and Bonaparte, which ended thus: "Considering that the brothers Bonaparte have succeeded in their efforts, and supported the impostures of the Arena, by joining the Commissioners of the Convention, who despair of subjecting us to their tyrannical factions, and threaten to sell us to the Genoese, considering on the other side that it is beneath the dignity of the Corsican people to trouble themselves about the families of Arena or Bonaparte, they abandon them to their own private remorse and to public opinion, which has already condemned them to perpetual execration and infamy."

The inhabitants of Ajaccio were less scrupulous. The dogs had received a bad name, and their fellow-citizens proceeded to hang them. The mansion of the Bonapartes was sacked, together with the houses of the Moltedo, of the Meuron, and of several other patriots. Letizia had a few days before received a letter from Napoleon. "Preparatevi, questo paese non é per noi." ("Prepare yourself; this country is not for us.") She retired with her children and Fesch to Milelli, where she was followed by the Abbé Coti and others. She tried to reach the tower of Campitello to join the squadron of the Commissioners, which she knew was expected. She travelled on a dark night, and with the greatest difficulty, guided through the tortuous paths and the brushwood by the faithful Lieutenant Nunzio Costa, gained Campitello on 21 May, the very day of the Commissioners' arrival.

Napoleon and Joseph, seeing some persons making signals on the beach, go to meet them in a boat, discover their mother and sisters, and conduct them to the ships. On 3 June the whole family were united in safety at Calvi.

These events brought about a complete rupture between Paoli and the Bonapartes. We need not dwell on the violent indictment which was drawn up by Napoleon against his former idol. Under the circumstances, strong language was, if not justifiable, excusable. The paper was carried to Paris by Joseph and laid before the Provisional Executive Council; Saliceti reached Paris at the same time and used similar language. On 17 July the Convention decreed that Paoli was a traitor to the republic. They declared him an outlaw, and placed under accusation Pozzo di Borgo and the leaders of the Paolist party. Angelo Chiappe did his best to defend the *babbo*, but he was not listened to. Saliceti gained a complete triumph, and the island was re-conquered. The future history of the island belongs to a period beyond the limits of this narrative. Paoli, to defend himself against the Convention, threw himself into the arms of the English. He longed to be viceroy, but the post was given to Sir Gilbert Elliot, and Elliot, under the influence of Pozzo, got rid of him. After Paoli had retired to London, Pozzo became the confidant and favourite of the viceroy. He left Corsica with Elliot, and entered the diplomatic service of Russia, where he remained the bitter enemy of Napoleon, whom he eventually succeeded in crushing. He is known to have fomented the bad feeling between Napoleon and Alexander, and he directed the policy of the allies in 1814.

Paoli was more generous. He was always proud of the successes of Napoleon. He called him "il nostro patriotto, il nostro nazionale." When eventually Corsica, by the influence of Napoleon, obtained liberty and good laws together with France, to which she belonged, he said, "Liberty was always the object of our revolution; the Corsicans now possess it, and it matters little from whose hands it has come. We have the happiness to have acquired it by one of our compatriots, who with so much honour and glory has vindicated our country from the injuries which almost all nations have cast upon us. I love him because he has shown that the inhabitants of the island, oppressed and misunderstood, can distinguish themselves in every career of life when they are once delivered from the cold hands of a tyrannical government. He has executed vengeance on all those who have been the cause of our abasement. The name of Corsica is now no longer despised, and we shall see still more of her sons figuring in the great theatre of Europe, for they have with them talent, a noble ambition and the bright example of Bonaparte."

Napoleon, on his side, was equally magnanimous. He was deeply touched by the expressions of Paoli. He said that he was a great man on a little stage, one of those rare geniuses which are suited to regenerate a degraded people. He said at Saint Helena that it had been one of his plans to attract Paoli from England, and to give him a share of his power. "It would have been," he said, "a great pleasure for me, and a real trophy."

CHAPTER XII

LE SOUPER DE BEAUCAIRE

When the Bonapartes were driven out of Ajaccio they took refuge with the Giubega family at Calvi. But it was impossible for them to stay in Corsica, and on 11 June they embarked for Toulon. At the end of the month they settled in the village of La Valette, at the gates of that town, but after a short stay removed to Marseilles. During this time Napoleon went to Nice to join his regiment, the headquarters being at Grenoble, but five companies being at Nice, under the command of Dujardin. He received, on his arrival, a commission as capitaine commandant. His company was called No. 12, but his gunners, following the custom of the *ancien régime*, called it the Bonaparte company. Napoleon found at Nice, commanding the artillery of the army of Italy, Jean, Chevalier du Teil, brother of the Baron du Teil who had been so kind to him on a previous occasion. Du Teil had been inspecting the shores of the Mediterranean and sketching a plan for defending the coast. He attached Napoleon to the service of the coast batteries, and on 3 July Napoleon requested, in his name, the military authorities, to furnish a model of a furnace for heating cannon balls better than those previously in use. A few days later he was sent to Avignon to superintend the convoys of powder which were passing to the army of Italy. At this time the Marseillais, who had risen in insurrection, were occupying Avignon, and an army commanded by Carteaux was marching to meet them. But when Napoleon arrived they had already evacuated the town, and Carteaux was pursuing them towards Marseilles. Bonaparte was at this time somewhat disappointed at not being employed on active service, and at the end of August he wrote to the Minister of War, Bouchotte, to request the rank of lieutenant-colonel and permission to serve in the army of the Rhône. Bouchotte did not answer, but he asked the local authorities to see the young officer and to promote him if he were deserving.

Napoleon now published a dialogue referring to the defeat of the federalists, entitled "The Supper at Beaucaire; or, a dialogue between a soldier of Carteaux's army, a Marseillais, a Nimois, and a manufacturer of Montpellier, on the events which have taken place in the combat (as it was familiarly called) on the arrival of the Marseillais."

He afterwards entitled it simply *Souper de Beaucaire*. The soldier was obviously Napoleon himself, there was a second Marseillais present, but he does not appear to have said anything. They are supposed to meet on the first day of the fair of Beaucaire, and as the manufacturer of Montpellier only speaks twice, and the Nimois only three times, the conversation is carried on almost exclusively between the soldier and the Marseillais.

After a few introductory remarks, the Marseillais asserts that his countrymen will in a few days be able to retake Avignon, or at least to remain master of the Durance. The soldier warns him of the danger that he is incurring of destroying the most beautiful town in France. "You were led to encourage all kinds of hopes which turned out to be false. You were led astray by self-love and by an exaggerated view of the services which you had rendered to liberty. Your army will be beaten; you can only collect five or six thousand men, without training or unity. You may have good guards, but they have no worthy subordinates. Carteaux, on the other hand, has excellently trained soldiers, accustomed to victory. You have some large cannons, but any experienced person will tell you that smaller guns would be equally efficacious. Your gunners are inexperienced, while those of Carteaux are among the best in Europe. If your army remains at Aix it will certainly be beaten, if it marches to meet the enemy it will be broken without reserve, for the cavalry will break it up. If you think of fighting at Marseilles itself, remember that a large body there is in favour of the republic; they will join Carteaux, and your town, the centre of the commerce of the East, the *entrepôt* of the south, is lost. How can you be mad enough and blind enough to resist the whole force of the republic? Even supposing you gained a temporary victory, new reinforcements would arrive. The republic which gives the law to Europe is not likely to receive it from Marseilles. Joined with Bordeaux, Lyons, Montpellier, Nîmes, Grenoble, the Jura, the Loire, the Calvados, you began a revolution which had a chance of success, but now that Lyons, Nimes, Montpellier, Bordeaux, the Jura, the Loire, Grenoble, and Caen have received the Constitution, and that Avignon, Tarascon, and Arles have yielded, your obstinacy becomes madness. You are exposing the flower of your youth to be maimed by old veterans accustomed to the blood of the aristocrats and the Prussians. Leave this kind of struggle to poor countries like the

Vivarais, Cevennes, and Corsica. They have little to lose, but if you lose a little, the fruit of a thousand years of toil, savings, and happiness becomes the prey of the soldier."

The Marseillais suggests that perhaps Provence will arise spontaneously and envelop the Republican army and force it to pass the Durance. The soldier replies that the two parties exist everywhere, and that the partisans of the sections will always prevail. "At Tarascon, Orgon, and Arles twenty dragoons have been sufficient to replace the former administration, and to expel the others. Henceforth no great movement in your favour is possible in your department. At Toulon the sectionaires are not so strong as at Marseilles, and they must stay in the town to keep the others down." The soldier then undertakes to defend the Republicans against the tirade of the Marseillais. "The Allobroges, whom do you think they are? Africans or Siberians? Not at all; they are compatriots, men of Provence, and Dauphiné, and Savoy; you think them barbarians because their name is strange. People in the same way might call you Phoceans. The soldiers which you call brigands are our best and most disciplined troops, Dubois-Crancé, and Albitte are constant friends of the people who have never deviated from the straight path. Condorcet, Brissot, Barbaroux were always considered villains when they were pure; it is the privilege of the good always to have a bad reputation in the eyes of the bad. You call Carteaux an assassin when he has done his utmost to preserve order and discipline, but your army killed men and assassinated more than thirty persons. Shake off the yoke of the small number of aristocrats who lead you, resume sounder principles, and you will never have truer friends than the soldiers."

The Marseillais observes that the army has much degenerated since 1769; it would not then have turned its arms against citizens. "Then," replies the soldier, "Vendée would have planted the white flag on the rebuilt Bastille, and the Camp de Jalès would rule at Marseilles." "Vendée and Jalès," says the interlocutor, "represented Royalists; we are Republicans, friends of law and order, enemies of anarchy and of villains. Have we not the tricolour flag?" "Yes," replies the soldier. "Paoli raised the tricolour flag in Corsica, so as to gain time to deceive the people, to crush the true friends of liberty, to be able to drag his countrymen into his ambitious and criminal projects. He hoisted the tricolour flag and he fired on the vessels of the republic; he drove our troops from their fortresses and drained their garrisons; he did his best to drive the rest of the troops from the island; he pillaged the magazines, selling everything in them at a low price, in order to get money to sustain his rebellion; he plundered and confiscated the property of the most prosperous families because they were attached to the unity of the republic, and he declared all those who remained in our armies enemies of our country; he had previously caused the expedition to Corsica to fail, and yet he had the confidence to declare himself a friend of France and a good Republican while he was deceiving the Convention which annulled the decree which deposed him. He acted so cleverly that when he was unmasked by his own letters found at Calvi, the time was past, and the enemy's fleet intercepted all communications."

We may suppose that Napoleon believed all this about Paoli at the time; but he had not always thought so, and the judgments here contained were expressed under a feeling of severe irritation. The conversation then turned on the character of the Girondists, Brissot, Barbaroux, Condorcet, Vergniaud, and Guadet. The soldier continues, "I do not ask whether the men who deserved so well of the people on so many occasions really conspired against the people; it is enough for me to know that when the Mountain, led by public and by party spirit, had proceeded to the last extremities against them, having condemned and imprisoned them, I will even admit having calumniated them, they were lost when a civil war broke out, which put them in a position to give the law to their enemies. Your war served their purpose. If they had deserved their precious reputation, they would have thrown away their arms at the sight of the Constitution, and would have sacrificed their interests to the public good; but it is more easy to praise Decius than to imitate him. They are shown today to be guilty of the greatest of all crimes, and have justified their condemnation by their conduct. The blood which they have caused to be shed has effaced the real services which they rendered." Napoleon here speaks like a true statesman, and what he says gives the key of his actions in Corsica. He may have sympathized with the Gironde more than with the Mountain, with Paoli more than with Saliceti; but the one necessity was to avoid civil war at all hazards, and to preserve intact the majesty and power of France. France might be led astray, but she would recover her senses; a civil war would tear her in pieces, and surrender her to the power of her enemies.

The manufacturer of Montpellier then enters into a long tirade against the conduct of Marseilles, which is put into his mouth, because Napoleon did not wish to make himself responsible for everything contained in it. At the close the Marseillais threatens that, if driven to extremity, his compatriots will surrender their country to Spain. The soldier shows the futility of this expedient, and the Marseillais concludes by avowing that their situation is desperate. "Well, sir, where is our remedy to be found? Is it in the refugees who come to us from all quarters of the departments? It is their interest to act as desperate men. Is it they who govern us?

Are they not in the same position? Is it the people? One faction does not understand its own position: is blinded, is frantic; the other is disarmed, suspected, humiliated. I see with profound affliction that our misfortunes have no remedy."

The soldier then terminates the discussion by saying, "At last you are reasonable. Why should not a similar change of opinion take place in the large number of your fellow-citizens who are deceived, and are yet of good faith? Then Albitte, who must be desirous to spare the blood of Frenchmen, will send you a man both loyal and adroit. You will be again of one mind, and the army, without halting for a single moment, will advance to the walls of Perpignan, to make the Spaniard, who has been elevated by a little success, dance the Carmagnole. Marseilles will then continue to be the centre of gravity of liberty. It will only be necessary to leave out a few pages from her history." Napoleon adds, "This prophecy put us all into good humour again. The Marseillais willingly paid for some bottles of champagne, which entirely dissipated our cares and anxieties. We went to bed at two in the morning, promising to meet again at breakfast the next day, when the Marseillais would again propose some difficulties, and I should teach him some interesting truths."

This paper is very remarkable. It is admirably written, and, notwithstanding some exaggerations, is full of sound good sense and political wisdom. But it attracted no attention. It was regarded as a party pamphlet, which the soldiers of Carteaux distributed in their march in answer to the similar leaflets of the departmental army. The quarrel had reached a stage beyond the power of argument. It had to be decided, not by the pen, but by the sword, and to be recorded in characters of fire and blood.

CHAPTER XIII

TOULON

Napoleon returned from Avignon to Nice, and on 15 September he wrote from Marseilles, ordering the authorities of Vaucluse to furnish five wagons for the transport of powder, intended not only for the service of the coast, but also for the army of Italy. At this time Toulon had rebelled against the Convention, and had delivered itself to the English, and the army of Carteaux had instructions to reduce it to obedience. On 7 September, he occupied the ravine of Ollioules, a gorge through which passes the only carriageable road between Toulon and Marseilles. In the action one man was killed and two were wounded, one of whom was Dommartin, the commander of the artillery. He was hit by a ball on the shoulder, as he was pointing a gun. By a kind of accident Napoleon was sent to replace him, and this proved an important epoch in his fortunes. At this time all armies in the field were attended by members of the Convention, and the two deputies attached to the army of Carteaux were Saliceti and Gasparin, who behaved admirably, and befriended Napoleon. Toulon was regarded at this time as one of the largest and most formidable fortresses in the world, the advanced works making the town impregnable. Its existing defences were strengthened by the English, who erected a number of new batteries. Carteaux, who commanded in chief, placed his headquarters at Ollioules, and directed the operations of the right division; whereas the left division was under the order of La Poype. On 18 September, two days after Napoleon's arrival, Carteaux drove the enemy from the Valley of Favières, seized the chateau of Dardennes, together with the foundry and the mills which supplied Toulon, and cut off their supply of water. After this the two divisions came closer together. The communications of Toulon with the interior were interrupted, and the only roads open were those of Ollioules on the west, and La Vallette on the east. Carteaux's army was not in a good condition. On 18 September it numbered ten thousand combatants, and it was constantly receiving reinforcements. But some of the battalions were not armed at all, and others did not know how to use their arms. There were some good troops; but even these took their duties easily. Artillery scarcely existed. Napoleon, when he arrived at Ollioules, found only two 24-pounders, two 16-pounders, and two mortars, and no ammunition or tools. The men were not much better than their pieces. The first care of Napoleon was to secure for the artillery more consideration and independence, and with that view he asked for a special general to command the artillery. La Salette, an old friend of Napoleon's, was chosen; but by an accident he did not reach Toulon till the town had been taken. Until the general should arrive, Napoleon insisted on taking his place. "Do your duty," he said to his colleagues, "and let me do mine." Three days after his arrival he had raised the strength of his arm to the number of four cannons, four mortars, and the materials for the construction of several batteries. On 18 October he was promoted to the rank of Chef de Bataillon.

To secure the success of the siege, the chief point was to compel the retirement of the English fleet. Immediately, on his arrival, Napoleon saw that this could be effected by seizing the point of L'Éguillette, which commands both roadsteads of Toulon—the larger and the smaller. If the Republicans could establish themselves on the promontory of Caire, they would render the roadsteads impassable; and the fleet once got rid of, Toulon was taken. This idea struck Saliceti and Gasparin most favourably; but they had to reckon with Carteaux. Carteaux had served in the army from his childhood, and had performed excellent service, but he was not intelligent, and knew nothing of the science of war. He delighted to exhibit himself in a blue coat covered with gold lace, twisting his large black moustache, proud of his fine face and clear complexion; but he would not recognize the importance of L'Éguillette, and preferred to place his guns in a casual manner. His idea was to attack Toulon in five different places and to take the forts by the bayonet. The bayonet was his favourite weapon. He consented, however, to occupy the promontory of Caire, and for this purpose it was necessary to capture the village of La Seyne.

On the evening of 17 September, the day after his arrival, Napoleon collected all the heavy artillery he could find. He then erected a new battery, called "La Batterie de la Montagne," and on 19 September he drove away a frigate and two pontoons anchored off La Seyne. That same night he erected another battery on the sea-coast, called "La Batterie des Sans Culottes." All the vessels of the English fleet opened fire upon it, but Napoleon replied with vigour, and the enemy's fleet had to keep their distance. He wrote to Marmont in 1798, "You remember our batteries at Toulon; artillery persistently served with red-hot cannon-balls is terrible against a fleet." The way was now clear for the occupation of La Seyne and L'Éguillette. "Take L'Éguillette," said Napoleon to Carteaux, "and within a week you are in Toulon." La Seyne was occupied by Delaborde on 21 September, and on the following day, at five p.m., he marched on L'Éguillette. But Carteaux had only given him four hundred men, and sent him no reinforcements; neither he nor Delaborde realized the importance of the position. The English sent reinforcements, and after a few minutes Delaborde retreated. The English now became aware of the importance of the place, and they erected a fort on the summit of the promontory, which they called Fort Mulgrave, while the French named it "the little Gibraltar," and the same day they erected three redoubts to support it. Napoleon was furious. He said, "The enemy have discovered the insufficiency of their marine artillery; they have captured a position, and they have cannon, a covered army, and pallisades; they will receive considerable reinforcements; there is nothing before us but a siege." At the same time he did not give up his idea.

He spared no efforts to prepare for the attack of L'Éguillette, and to get together the siege train. His activity was prodigious. He heaped order upon order, and requisition upon requisition, draining everything he could from the neighbouring towns, taking from Martigues eight bronze cannon, which he replaced by eight iron cannon, drawing from the citadels of Antibes and Monaco guns which he considered useless for their defence, taking from La Seyne and La Ciotat the wood and the piles which were necessary to build platforms for the cannons and mortars, getting together from all the departments from Nice to Montpellier draught oxen and other animals, organizing brigades of wagoners, obtaining from Marseilles every day a hundred thousand sacks of earth, employing basket-makers to make gabions, erecting at Ollioules an arsenal of eighty forges and a workshop for repairing muskets. His choice of subordinates was not less happy, and he contrived to inspire them with his own enthusiasm. He succeeded with some difficulty in securing the services of Gassendi, his old comrade in the regiment of La Fère, whose hatred of the crimes of the Revolution was well known, and but for Napoleon's insistence, would have prevented his employment.

Napoleon was in great need of powder, which was absolutely necessary for the operations. He protested against the soldiers' waste of cartridges, and the indifference of his superiors. He continued to fight hard for the independence of the artillery. He exhibited the utmost bravery, and exposed his life with the greatest coolness. One day he took the ramrod of a gunner who had fallen, and used it ten or twelve times; unfortunately the fallen gunner had a disagreeable skin complaint, which Napoleon contracted to the injury of his health for some time. The siege train arrived duly from Marseilles. Napoleon constructed several batteries, the best known being the Batterie des Sans Culottes, already mentioned, north of La Seyne. This was armed with a large 44-pounder, which had a great reputation for doing damage. But it was of an antiquated pattern, and was found to be of no use. The battery was, however, armed with one 36-pounder, four 24-pounders, and a 12-pounder mortar. The result was to sweep the enemy's fleet from the western part of the great roadstead and to keep it at a respectful distance.

On 1 October, La Poype, against the wishes of Carteaux, attacked Mount Faron. He succeeded in occupying it, but was intercepted in his retreat by Lord Mulgrave and Gravina, and was completely defeated. This encouraged the besieged, who made a sortie on the night of 8 October, in which they took a French artillery lieutenant prisoner. He wrote to Napoleon to say that he was well treated, and the letter was published in the *Journal d'Avignon*. It is said that this is the first time that the name of Napoleon appeared in a public print. A still more important sortie was made on 14 October, in the direction of Ollioules, but Napoleon came to the rescue, and the assailants were driven back. Here he fought against English troops, and recognized their merit. On the following day, La Poype occupied Cap Brun, but was not able to retain it.

Napoleon was disgusted with the slowness of the siege and the bad discipline of the army, many of the officers going to amuse themselves at Marseilles. Reinforcements were urgently demanded from the government at Paris, but without effect. La Poype and Carteaux were not on speaking terms, and were always girding at each other. Saliceti and Gasparin became convinced of the incapacity of Carteaux, their eyes being opened by the complaints of Napoleon. Among other incidents he reported that, when he had first shown Carteaux the importance of L'Éguillette, and placing his finger upon it had said, "Toulon is there," Carteaux poked the man standing next to him with his elbow, and remarked, "Here is a fellow who is not very strong in geography." Napoleon even proceeded to actual disobedience. Carteaux having ordered him to erect a battery which would attack three English forts, Napoleon pointed out that to secure success it would be necessary to attack one English fort with three or four batteries, and that to build a fort which would be destroyed in a quarter of an hour by superior force would be worse than useless. On a second occasion he refused to construct a battery in a position where there was no room for the recoil of the guns. Napoleon told Gasparin that he would not serve under a man who was wanting in the most elementary notions of the military art. Carteaux's wife was more sensible than himself. She said, "Let this young man alone; he knows more than you. He asks nothing from you, he is responsible to you. If he succeeds the glory is yours, if he fails the blame will be his." Carteaux took her advice, and told "Captain Cannon," as he called Napoleon, that he must answer for his plan with his head. He, however, lost his self-control in saying to the Jacobins of Marseilles, "The artillery will not obey me, and its commander Bonaparte has some secret end in view which I have not yet discovered, but to attack the head of the artillery is to attack the representatives." At last Carteaux was recalled. Barras, Frèron, and Augustin Robespierre added their complaints to those of Saliceti and Gasparin, and Ricord took them to Paris in person. On 23 October Carteaux was ordered to join the headquarters of the army of Italy at Nice. He was very unwilling to obey, as he desired to beat the English and to take Toulon, but he left on 7 November, and Doppet, his successor, did not arrive till 12 November, during which time the command was exercised by La Poype.

The real commander, however, was Saliceti, who was devoted to Napoleon. Gasparin, worn out with fatigue, retired to Orange, where he died. Doppet was a native of Savoy, who had been a doctor at Chambéry, and since the outbreak of the Revolution a writer at Paris. He had distinguished himself as commander of the legions of the Allobroges, and had been made general as a reward, and sent to the conquest of Lyons. After the reduction of the Lyonese, he had been despatched to Toulon because it was thought that he would bring with him large reinforcements. He had more ability than Carteaux, but had no military knowledge. He was, however, conscious of his own deficiencies. On 15 November he had a good chance of taking Toulon by an accident. A French battalion posted opposite Fort Mulgrave, seeing one of their countrymen, who had been taken prisoner, ill-treated by Spaniards, rushed to attack the fort; other battalions came up, and then a whole division. A hot combat was engaged. Doppet and Bonaparte hastened to the scene of action. Napoleon thought it was better to go on than to withdraw, and Doppet allowed him to command. Napoleon forced two companies of grenadiers to enter Fort Mulgrave by a ravine. General O'Hara, the English commandant of the town, who saw the engagement from the deck of the *Victory*, rushed to the spot to encourage his troops, and a sortie was made from the fort, which was vigorously supported by the batteries and the ships. Doppet saw his *aide-de-camp* killed at his side, and ordered the retreat. Napoleon was beside himself with rage, and galloped up to Doppet and said, "We have lost Toulon." The soldiers complained, "Shall we always be commanded by painters and doctors?"

Doppet was sent to the army of the Pyrenees, Carteaux to the army of the Alps, and the command was given to Dugommier, with special instructions to carry on the siege of Toulon with vigour. He arrived at Ollioules on 16 November; two hours later the younger Du Teil came to command the artillery, and a week later Marescot took charge of the engineers. At the same time large reinforcements both of men and material reached the place. Jacques Coquille Dugommier was fifty-five years of age, tall, with an open countenance, burned by the sun, a high forehead, piercing and fiery eyes, and thick white hair, forming altogether an imposing personality which had great influence on the soldiers. He did much to establish discipline, and quickly appreciated the talent of Bonaparte. It is said that once when Napoleon was dining as his guest he offered him a dish of brains, saying, "Eat these, for you need them;" meaning, not that Napoleon was deficient in brains, but that he had work enough to employ all the brains he had, and more still. Du Teil was in bad health, and left everything to his subordinate. Dugommier soon became convinced that he had not sufficient resources to undertake a regular siege. On 25 November he held a council of war which was attended by Robespierre, Ricord, and Saliceti, La Poype, Mouret, and Du Teil, La Barre and Garnier, Bonaparte, Sugny, and Brûlé. He said that he had only twenty-five thousand fighting men, and that his supply of powder was very deficient. Two plans were submitted to the meeting. Dugommier urged the capture of Fort Mulgrave, L'Éguillette, and Belaguier, which would have the effect of driving the enemy from the smaller into the larger roadstead. Mortars were to be placed at Cap Brun, Faron and Malbousquet seized, and the town attacked. Carnot's plan was that the army should be divided into two columns, that the first was to seize Cap Brun and the second L'Éguillette and Belaguier, that batteries firing red-hot balls were to be placed on the peninsula of Croix aux Signaux, and that the town was to be set on fire. Dugommier thought that his army was not large enough to attack the peninsula; the council were of opinion that it would be impossible to attack Cap Brun. It was eventually decided to make a false attack upon Cap Brun and Malbousquet, and a real attack on Fort Mulgrave, L'Éguillette, Belaguier, and Mount Faron. This was the plan of Bonaparte, who drew up the minutes of the sitting.

At this time there were three batteries directed against Fort Malbousquet, two against the little roadstead, five against L'Éguillette and the Grand

Roadstead, and three in front of all the others, called by the names of "Les Republicains du Midi," "Les Chasse-Coquins," and "Les Hommes Sans Peur." This last was armed by three 16-pounders and five mortars, and it had also a bomb-proof powder magazine. The remains of it are still to be distinguished in the brushwood. It was the most exposed of all the batteries, and its construction was forbidden by Carteaux, because he believed it untenable. At first it was found impossible to man it; but Napoleon, who knew the French character, set up a signpost with the inscription written by Junot, "Batterie des Hommes-sans-Peur," so that it was sought after by the bravest gunners in the force. This battery opened fire on 22 November.

The battery which did most injury to the besieged was the "Batterie de la Convention," which was directed against Fort Malbousquet. O'Hara determined to silence it, and on the morning of 30 November he collected 2,350 men, English, Sardinians, Neapolitans, Spaniards, and French under the orders of Major-General Dundas, behind the Riviere Neuve, between the Forts of Malbousquet and Saint-Antoine. They passed the river by a single bridge, divided into four columns, and appeared suddenly on the plateau; the troops pushed into the batteries and spiked the guns. General Garnier tried to rally his men, but they were scattered by the fire of Malbousquet, the allies pushed on in the direction of Ollioules, and it seemed as if they would attack the artillery park. At this moment Dugommier, accompanied by Saliceti, arrived on the scene. He checked the fugitives with words and blows, and eventually found himself in sufficient force to retake the plateau. The allies, who had imprudently scattered, began to retreat and were eventually put to flight. General O'Hara was at the Batterie de la Convention when he saw his men retreating. He ran to meet the Republican forces, but was wounded in the arm, and was compelled by loss of blood to sit down at the foot of a wall. Here he was made prisoner. The allies retired to Malbousquet pursued by the French led by Mouret, who unwisely tried to capture the fort, and did not return to camp till nightfall. Napoleon took the spikes out of the guns, and opened fire on Malbousquet. He reported the same evening, "The fort replied vigorously and killed a sergeant of artillery, but our soldiers marched on Malbousquet and advanced as far as the chevaux de frise. We drove the enemy from two contiguous heights, we destroyed an earthwork which they were beginning to make, we carried off a large number of tents, and destroyed those which we could not carry away." Dugommier and Napoleon were delighted at the results of the day. What might they not expect from a concerted attack, when an accidental dash succeeded so well. Dugommier wrote on the following day to the Minister of War that Bonaparte, Commander of Artillery, and the Adjutants-General Arena and Cervoni had distinguished themselves greatly, and had been of the greatest assistance in rallying the troops and in pushing them forward. Saliceti said, "Our soldiers would perform prodigies, if they only had officers. Dugommier, Garnier, Mouret, and Bonaparte behaved very well." In the evening, Bonaparte, by the wish of Dugommier, paid a visit to the prisoner O'Hara, and asked what he wanted. "To be left alone, and to owe nothing to pity," was O'Hara's reply. Napoleon did not think much of O'Hara as a general, but he praised his reply. "A conquered prisoner," he said, "should act with reserve and pride, and neither wish nor ask for anything." Napoleon certainly followed these precepts when he found himself in a similar position. O'Hara was not released till August, 1795.

The engagement of 30 November only cost the Republicans 300 men, but it revealed their weakness. The left wing of the army had been cut to pieces without making the slightest resistance, and about 600 brave soldiers, led by still braver officers, had conquered positions which a division of 6,000 men had lost in an instant. On that day, Dugommier tells us, the French army had used 500,000 cartridges, and with no result whatever. Napoleon still kept his eyes fixed on Fort Mulgrave, which was armed by twenty guns and four mortars, and was garrisoned by 700 soldiers, with 2,200 men and a battery of six pieces to support it. At the same time Toulon appeared to be impregnable, and even Barras and Fréron began to believe that the enterprise was hopeless. Dugommier felt that he must strike a final blow, but he hesitated, because he knew that the guillotine awaited him if he failed. At the very moment when he was marching to the assault of Fort Mulgrave he whispered to Victor, "We must take the redoubts; if not——" and he passed his hand across his throat. He did not like to act until he had received all the reinforcements which were promised to him by the Minister of War and the Committee. But the reinforcements did not arrive, and when they did were of little use.

On 11 December another council of war was held at Ollioules, in which it was decided to execute the plan of attack which had been determined upon on 25 November. Dugommier took Napoleon's view of the primary importance of L'Éguillette. The French, once master of that promontory, would compel the English to evacuate the harbour and the roadstead, and the departure of the fleet would fill the town with consternation. It was determined to use every effort to capture Fort Mulgrave, and at the same time to attack Mount Faron and other points. On 14, 15 and 16

December Fort Mulgrave was mainly bombarded by five French batteries. Dundas, who had succeeded O'Hara in the command, recognized that serious damage had been done to the works, and he sent a reinforcement of three hundred men to the promontory. It was eventually determined to attack Fort Mulgrave with seven thousand men, specially chosen. At one a.m. on the morning of 17 December the attacking party was formed into three columns—the first, commanded by Victor, was to march round the shore; the second, under the order of Brûlé, was to approach the promontory on the left and attack the redoubts in front; the third was to act as reserve. The commander of the artillery was to provide a full supply of ammunition for the mortars and red-hot cannonballs. Dugommier specially recommended order, self-control, and silence. On 16 December the troops came together in admirable temper, but the weather was stormy, and the rain fell in torrents. The Commissioners of the Executive were in favour of delaying the attack, and Dugommier was inclined to put it off till the following day. But Napoleon declared that the bad weather was favourable to their plans, and animated their spirits for the attack, which began at one a.m. However, the darkness and the rain induced confusion, and the two attacking columns took the main route, while many also went astray in the night. Indeed, the second column broke up with cries of "Sauve qui peut" and "À la trahison." But the seasoned troops advanced shoulder to shoulder, gained the foot of the promontory, mounted the slope, drove back a large body of English and an outpost of Spaniards, and in the midst of storm and thunder, and a hail of cannon-balls, speedily approached, reached the fort, tore down the chevaux de frise, crossed the abattis and the ditch, scaled the parapet, killed or wounded the gunners, and entered the redoubt with cries of "Victoire! à la baionette." Here they unexpectedly met with new earthworks, and were compelled to retire. A second time they advanced, and a second time they were driven back. Dugommier cried, "I am ruined." He then went to the reserve, commanded by Napoleon. A battalion of chasseurs, led by Muiron, who knew the ground well, came up immediately, mounted the height, and at three a.m. the redoubt was taken. Muiron was the first to enter, then Dugommier, and then Napoleon. The bayonets did the work, and the English gunners were cut down at their guns. There was not a single English prisoner who had not received a wound. It was a contest between English steadiness and French vivacity.

Napoleon had greatly distinguished himself. His horse was shot under him on leaving the village of La Seyne, and an Englishman wounded him with a bayonet in the thigh. He afterwards said, on board the *Northumberland*, that he had received his first wound from an Englishman. The guns of the forts were now turned against the enemy under the direction of Marmont. When day broke, the French columns marched against L'Éguillette and Belaguier; they found that the enemy had evacuated these two places, having killed their horses and mules. Bonaparte tried to fire at the fleet, but he found that for this purpose new batteries were necessary. In the meantime considerable advantages had been gained on the side of Mount Faron. Napoleon went to the battery of the Convention to attack Malbousquet, but he knew that the capture of L'Éguillette had decided the fate of the town, and he cried, "Tomorrow or the next day we shall sup in Toulon." In fact, during the morning of 17 December, the allies, recognizing that their line of defence was broken and that they could not secure the positions which they had lost, hastened to leave a city which had become untenable. If they delayed, the strong winds would prevent them leaving the harbour. In the evening the English fleet retired to the end of the Grand Roadstead, and on the following morning the French found that all the principal forts had been evacuated, the only one remaining occupied being Fort Mulgrave, which protected the embarkation of the garrison. The inhabitants began a precipitate flight; they strained every effort to gain the allied fleet, and many were drowned. At nine p.m. there was a terrible explosion which shook the town to its foundations. Sidney Smith, who was afterwards to repel Napoleon from St Jean d'Acre, set fire to a large part of the arsenal, the magazine, and twelve vessels of the French fleet. This terrible spectacle was never effaced from the memory of Napoleon.

The French entered the town on 19 December, and then began the terrible reprisals which have covered the capture of Toulon with infamy. Napoleon witnessed with horror excesses which he was powerless to prevent, and he took no part in the massacres which were ordered by Barras and Frèron. We have the testimony of eyewitnesses, that he did his best to save the victims, and that he moved about amidst the slaughter grave and silent, a stranger to the terrible scenes of which he disapproved. None of the cannon under his orders were used to slaughter the unfortunate inhabitants. He armed his batteries and destroyed an English frigate. He found that no French cannon had been spiked by the allies, and that the damage done in the arsenal was reparable. They had retired in such haste that, besides munitions of war, they had left fifteen ships to be used by the republic. After this narrative, we need not dwell on the service which Napoleon rendered during the siege, nor on the flattering testimonials which he received. Du Teil wrote to Bouchotte, the

Minister of War, "I have no words to describe the merit of Bonaparte: much science, as much intelligence, and too much bravery. This is but a feeble sketch of the qualities of this rare officer, and it is for you, ministers, to consecrate him to the glory of the Republic." On 22 November 1793, the Commissioner of the Convention appointed Napoleon general of brigade, "For the zeal and intelligence of which he has given proof in contributing to the surrender of the rebel town." On 1 February 1794, this appointment was confirmed by the Provisional Government. It can also be shown, by irrefragable evidence, that there was not a person who came under Napoleon's notice at Toulon who did not, in after years, receive some reward for his services. Even Carteaux received a special pension of 6,000 francs, and his widow one of 3,000. "To have been before Toulon" was always a passport to Napoleon's generosity, although he was often met by ingratitude.

We will say nothing of Victor, of Suchet, of Desaix, of Marmont, of Junot, because their fame belongs to the history of France and of Europe, except that it may be worthwhile to repeat the story which tells how Junot first attracted the attention of his patron. One day, before Toulon, Napoleon, wishing to dictate an order, called for someone who could write a good hand, and Junot, being famous in this respect, was presented to him. He was writing on the earthwork of the battery, when a cannonball covered himself and his papers with earth. "Good," said Junot, "we shall not require any sand." From that moment Napoleon attached him to his service. Jean Baptiste de Muiron demands a special notice. He was the son of a former general, and was fortunate enough to save his father from prison during the Terror. He had a charming face, and an outward appearance of frivolity and vanity which seemed likely to exclude him from serious employment. Napoleon met him at Toulon, and made him chief of his staff. In 1796 he held at bay for forty-eight hours the army of Würmser, which was endeavouring to enter Venice. Napoleon made him his *aide-de-camp* on the same day as Duroc. He perished at the bridge of Arcola. Napoleon tells us, "He threw himself before me, covering me with his body, and received the stroke which was intended for me. He fell dead at my feet, and his blood spurted on to my face." Napoleon wrote to his wife, "You have lost a husband who was dear to you; I have lost a friend to whom I have been long attached; but our country loses more than both of us in losing an officer distinguished as much by his talent as by his rare courage." Napoleon persuaded the Directory to erase the names of the mother and brother of Muiron from the list of *emigés*. The frigate which took Napoleon back from Egypt was called the *Muiron*; he wished to have it preserved as a monument in the docks at Toulon, regarding it as a talisman. When he was contemplating flight to the United States in 1815, he desired to take the name of Muiron; and at St Helena, when the English Government refused him the title of Emperor, he requested that he might be called Baron Duroc or Colonel Muiron. In his will be left 100,000 francs to the widow, the son, or the grandsons of his former *aide-de-camp*.

Such was the young Napoleon, at an age when young Englishmen are just taking their degree. Born of a noble family but very poor, losing his father at an early age, with nothing but himself to depend upon, he had raised himself to the rank of general in the French army by no other arts than those of industry and steadfastness, high character and devotion to duty, supported, no doubt, by talents almost without example. In these first twenty-three years of his life there is not a single example of meanness or of dishonesty, or of any derogation from the high standard of conduct which he had set before himself. At Brienne, disgusted with the abandoned morals of those surrounding him, he was forced to hold himself aloof; but he made many friends, and was far from being the gloomy misanthrope which some biographers have declared him to have been. At Paris he was the life of a chosen circle, and he showed the same firmness in the selection of his friends, and the same courage in asserting his principles, which distinguished the whole of his youth. Whatever may have been his desire for personal advancement, his care for himself was at least equalled by his love of his family and of his native land. Thrown by accident into an epoch of Revolution, he trod the difficult path of safety with marvellous wisdom and self-command. If the idea of the regeneration and independence of Corsica ever occurred to him, he soon became convinced that the prosperity of his island was indissolubly bound up with its connection with France. Disapproving of the execution of the king and of the persecution of the Girondists, and sympathizing very little with the excesses of the Mountain, he saw that a patriotic Frenchman must follow the main course of French political feeling, and that any other action would lead to civil war. Some biographers have complained of his frequent leave and his absence from his regiment; but this behaviour must be judged by the standard of the custom of the time, and it never estranged the sympathy of those whose duty it was to decide upon his conduct. Arriving in France a fugitive and an exile, burdened with the heavy charge of an exiled family, he raised himself in a few months to a position which any officer might envy. Surely, in his case also, the youth is father of the man; and twenty-three years spent under the most difficult circumstances which could try the qualities of a character, crowned by high success legitimately gained, are not likely to have been followed by twenty-three other years stained by universal ambition, reckless duplicity, and an aimless lust of bloodshed. The contemplation of this laborious and brilliant youth may, perhaps, dispose Englishmen to look more favourably upon those epochs of his career when devotion to the interests of France made him, for a time, the most formidable enemy of our own country.

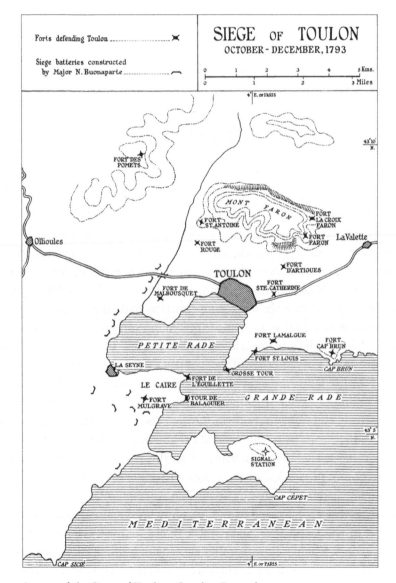

A map of the Siege of Toulon, October-December 1793.

APPENDIX I

A

CORSICA

26 April 1786.

Today Paoli enters upon his sixty-first year. Would his father, Hiacinto Paoli, ever have believed, when he came into the world, that he would be one day reckoned amongst the foremost men of modern Italy? The Corsicans were, in those unhappy times (in 1725), crushed more than ever by Genoese tyranny. More degraded than beasts, they dragged out in continual disorder an unhappy life, degrading for humanity. However, since 1715, some districts had taken arms against their tyrants; but it was not till 1729 that the revolution can properly bc said to have commenced, in which so many acts were performed of signal intrepidity and of a patriotism comparable to that of the Romans. Well! let us see, let us discuss a little. Had the Corsicans the right to shake off the Genoese yoke? Let us listen to the cry of prejudice: people are always wrong to revolt against their sovereigns. Divine law forbids it. What have divine laws to do with a matter purely human? But imagine the absurdity of this general prohibition, made by divine law, never to shake off the yoke, even of an usurper! By this reasoning an assassin, clever enough to obtain possession of thc throne, after the murder of the legitimate prince, is immediately protected by divine law, whereas, if he had not succeeded, bc would have been condemned to lose his guilty head upon the scaffold. Do not tell me that he will be punished in the other world, because I could say the same of all criminals. It would follow that they should not be punished in this one. It is, moreover, clear that a law is always independent of the success of the crime which it condemns.

As for human laws, they cannot exist as soon as the sovereign violates them. Either the people has set up these laws by submitting to the sovereign, or it is the sovereign himself who has set them up. In the first case, the sovereign is inviolably obliged to execute these conventions by the very nature of his sovereignty. In the second case, these laws ought to conduce to the end of government, which is the peace and happiness of the peoples. If the sovereign does not do this, it is obvious that the people return to a state of nature, and that the government, no longer contributing to the object of the social compact, is *ipse facto* dissolved; but further, the agreement by which a people places the sovereign authority in the hands of anybody whatever is not a contract—that is to say, the people may resume at will the sovereignty which they have delegated. Men in a state of nature do not form governments. To establish a government, each individual must consent to the change. The act which constitutes this convention is necessarily a reciprocal contract. The laws are made by all those who have entered into this engagement.

They were then in this position of sovereigns. Either by the difficulty of assembling frequently, or for some other reason, the people has committed its authority to a body or to a private individual. Now, no one is bound by engagements which he has contracted against his will. There are no preexisting laws which the people, who, in every government whatever, must he regarded as fundamentally sovereign, cannot abrogate. This does not apply to the relations which they may have with neighbouring nations.

Open the annals of Corsica, read the Memoirs of its brave inhabitants—those of Michele Merello, etc.,—but, much more, read the proposals of peace framed by the Republic itself, and, by the remedies which they apply, you will judge of the abuses which must have existed. You will see that the encroachments of the republic in the island were begun by the treason and the violation of the laws of hospitality, obtained by a ruse from Bonifacio and from the legislators of Cape Corso. You will see that they maintained, by the strength of their Navy, the false hopes of the inhabitants of the districts of Istria against the Republic of Pisa, who possessed a part of them. Finally, if by cunning, perfidy, and good luck they happened to make the estates consent to declare the republic of Genoa sovereign, you will see by the charter, so vaunted by the Corsicans, what were the conditions on which their sovereign principality was to be based. But to whatever nation you belong, even if you are an ex-eunuch of the harem, restrain, if you can, your indignation at the recital of the cruelties which they employed to maintain their power. Paolo, Colombano, Sampietro, Pompiliani, Gafforio illustrious avengers of humanity, heroes who delivered your compatriots from the rage of despotism, what was the recompense of your virtues? The dagger, yes, the dagger!

Effiminates of modern times, ye who spend your languid lives almost without exception in a silken slavery, these heroes are too far exalted above your cowardly minds; consider the picture of the young Leonardo, the youthful martyr of his country and of paternal love. What kind of death closed your heroic career in the springtime of your years? The gallows.

Men of the mountain, who has disturbed your happiness? Men of peace and virtue who spent your happy days in the bosom of your fatherland, what barbarous tyrant has destroyed your habitations? Four thousand families were forced to leave at a moment's notice. You, who have nothing but your country, by what unexpected event do I see you transplanted to foreign climes? The fire destroys your rustic abodes, and you no longer can hope to live with your household gods. Miserable Spinola! may the avenging furies make you expiate in the most horrible torments the murder of the Zucci, the Rafaelli, and the other illustrious patriots whom you had massacred in spite of the laws of hospitality which had summoned them into your palace. There was no kind of death which the republic hesitated to use in order to destroy the supporters of Corsican liberty.

If it is proved, by the nature of the social contract, that a nation may depose its sovereign without any reason; how does the case stand with regard to a private person, who, by violating all natural laws, by committing crimes and atrocities, goes against the principle for which government is instituted? Does not this course of reasoning apply specially to the Corsicans, since the sovereignty, or rather the principality, of the Genoese rested only upon convention. Thus the Corsicans were fully justified in getting rid of the Genoese, and may do the same with the French.

B

ON SUICIDE

Always alone in the midst of men, I come back to my rooms to dream with myself, and to surrender myself to all the vivacity of my melancholy. Towards which side is it turned today? To the side of death. In the dawn of my days, I can still hope to live a long time. I have been away from my country for about six or seven years. What pleasures shall I not enjoy, when in four months' time I see once more my compatriots and my relations? From the tender sensations with which the recollection of the pleasures of my childhood now fill me, may I not infer that my happiness will be complete? What madness leads me, then, to wish my death? Doubtless the thought: What is there to do in this world? Since I must die, is it not just as well that I should kill myself? If I had already passed my sixtieth year, I should respect the prejudices of my contemporaries, and wait patiently till nature had finished its course; but since I begin to experience misfortune, and since nothing is a pleasure to me, why should I support a life, in which nothing prospers for me? How far are men removed from nature! How cowardly they are, how abject, how servile! What spectacle shall I behold in my country? My fellow-countrymen loaded with chains, while they kiss with fear the hand that oppresses them! They are no longer those Corsicans, whom a hero inspired with his virtues, enemies to tyrants, of luxury, of demoralized towns. Proud, filled with a noble sentiment of his personal importance, a Corsican lived happy if he had passed the day in public affairs. The night was spent in the tender arms of a beloved wife. Reason and enthusiasm wiped out all the sorrows of the day. Love and nature made his nights resemble those of the gods. But with liberty they have vanished like dreams—those happy days. You Frenchmen, not content with having robbed us of everything we held dear, have also corrupted our character. The actual condition of my country, and the impossibility of changing it, is another reason for escaping from an earth, where I am obliged to praise men from a sense of duty, whom I must hate from a sense of virtue. When I arrive in my fatherland, what attitude am I to hold—what language am I to use? A good patriot ought to die when his fatherland has ceased to exist. If the deliverance of my fellow-countrymen depended upon the death of a single man, I would go immediately and plunge the sword which would avenge my country and its violated laws into the breast of tyrants. Life is a burden to me, because I enjoy no pleasure, and because everything is painful to me. It is a burden to me because the men with whom I live, and with whom I shall probably always live, are as different in character to myself as the brightness of the moon differs from that of the sun. The result is that I cannot follow the only kind of life which would make life endurable, and hence comes a disgust for everything.

C

THE REFUTATION OF M. ROUSTAN

May 9, 4 p.m.

Rousseau! one of your fellow-citizens, of your friends, a virtuous man, who declares that he is superior to the ordinary prejudices of mankind, would like to destroy the prejudices which he charges you with possessing with regard to religion considered on its political side. This is not due to passion, so often the secret motive of human actions. He is inspired, not by pride, hatred, or jealousy, but by sovereign truth. He bows before it, and, convinced of your respect for its sacred torch, he publishes his reflections on the eighth chapter of your *Contrat Social*. But no! there is no doubt that it is not enough to be virtuous and a lover of truth to contend against Rousseau. He was a man, and therefore I can easily believe that he did not see everything in its true light. The matter in dispute is not one of his isolated ideas, but one of the most important chapters of the *Contrat Social*, an idea which it is necessary to sound to the bottom in order to discover some portion of the difference which exists between modem and ancient govemments.

Is the Christian religion favourable for the political government of a State? Rousseau is so certain of his conclusions that he says "the third (meaning the Roman Catholic religion) is so evidently bad that it is waste of time to amuse oneself by proving it:' Everything which destroys social unity is of no value. All the institutions which place a man in contradiction to himself are worth nothing. As these principles are beyond dispute, M. Roustan cannot find fault with them, but he denies that reformed Catholic religions are in the same position. As far as the Roman Catholic religion is concerned, it is abundantly proved that the unity of the State is broken by it.

Let us carefully examine the arguments which he alleges against Rousseau. It is true that both Christianity and government have a common end, the happiness of mankind, but does it follow from this that the unity of the State is not injured by it? Doubtless it is. They arrive at the same end, but by opposite paths. Christianity makes men happy by the contempt which it inspires for the evils which afflict us in this world. "What is life in comparison with eternity?" I am miserable, and you, wretched man, are prosperous, but wait till we are both before the tribunal of the Supreme Being. Then the bill will become due, and will be settled once for all.

Government watches over the security of its subjects. "Thou hast injured me, thou hast broken my laws; come and render me an account before the minister of justice, the avenger of crime and the supporter of the law." You can clearly see, therefore, that the spirit which animates Christianity on the one side and government on the other, is different in each case, although they both attain the same end. But if, in one of those moments of crisis which arise in every State, it becomes necessary for an instant to make the people unhappy, in order to save the country, Christianity would oppose you and would impede the designs of govemment. This settles the question.

Christianity forbids men to obey every order which is contrary to its law, every unjust order, even if it comes from the people itself. In this way it contradicts the first article of the social compact, on which governments are based, for it substitutes its individual opinions for the general will which constitutes sovereignty. As we are considering this matter from a political point of view, we must take account of these drawbacks. The manner in which the Gospel forbids certain actions entirely destroys the unity of the State, because the ministers of the law and the ministers of religion are not the same. If the spirit of particularism which animates the latter body were carried to its strict conclusion, it would induce them to an indirect disobedience of the commands of the sovereign. In short, what is the tribunal which is to decide whether a certain order is unjust? Conscience, you say. But who directs the conscience? You see that in this case the State is no longer one. Follow this reasoning, and you will see that the reply of the Vicomte d'Orthe is very différent under a Christian government. You are yourself conscious of the influence which the ministers of religion may have against the law, since you advise that priests should be enlightened and virtuous in order to prevent abuses in elections. You perceive, then, that they have more influence in politics than even the ministers of the law. Therefore, as the ministers of religion, in their corporations, are never, or hardly ever, citizens, but always ministers, there must be a conflict of influences.

I will not point out a large number of real contradictions or inconsequences into which M. Roustan falls. I have mentioned enough of them. We may, then, consider it certain that Christianity, even when reformed, destroys the unity of the State, first, because it either increases or weakens the confidence which ought to be given to the ministers of the law, and secondly, because by its constitution it forms a separate body which not only divides the heart of the citizen, but, besides, may often oppose the views of the government. Besides, is not this body independent of the State? It is, because it is not governed by the same principles. Is it ever seen to defend the laws and liberty of its country? No. Its empire is not of this world. It is, therefore, never a citizen.

Given that Christianity destroys the unity of the State, may we infer that it has been the cause of so many troubles which have disturbed Christian States. Rousseau asserts this, and we must now examine it. Experience teaches us every day that the mind of fallible man, if it follow the tortuous paths of metaphysics, will go wrong in a view, a supposition, or a principle. But M. Roustan will have difficulty in persuading us that Jean Jacques, the author of *Émile* and of the *Contrat Social*, that deep and penetrating man, who employed his life in studying men; that Rousseau, who has so successfully unveiled the tiny springs of great affairs, has drawn a false conclusion, and has mistaken the principles which have delivered Christian States to all the fury of civil dissension. Nevertheless, do not let us be led away by enthusiasm. Who can thoroughly know the variability of the human mind? Many a doughty diver who has sounded the depths of the mighty ocean, who has seen without trembling the precipices which threatened his life, has ended it miserably in a peaceful bog. You must distinguish the spirit which Christianity gave by its constitution to the clergy, from the precise meaning of a law. Some one says, "You are more powerful than the sovereign himself, you have need of wealth to support your work, and to keep up your position amongst the other classes of the community." This voice, which always makes itself heard, soon prevails. The Gospel originally said to them, "Remain poor," but they speedily disregard the advice. It follows, then, that Rousseau only attacks the spirit of the constitution, which, by breaking the unity of the State and by making ministers of religion powerful, rich, and jealous for their intolerant dogmas, has been the cause of all the wars which have torn Christian States asunder. The charges which you lay against Christian empires you should rather bring against Christianity itself, because one follows naturally from the other. If opinions are divided about an article of faith, one only can be right, that of Jesus Christ. Each party supports his view with the same obstinacy. Disturbances arise from the desire to get the people on their side. Each side regards the other with horror, and seems to see on its forehead the punishment of hell. Which of the two will give way? They are prevented from acknowledging defeat, not only by a sense of shame and of self-love, but by the fear of losing credit, wealth, and the support of the people. The contest continues with obstinacy. A man who is not walking in the way of the Lord ought not to enjoy the advantage of His creatures. At any rate, he must be deprived of worldly property. What part will the ministers of the law play in all this? Will they offer to arbitrate between the two parties? What temerity! "What are you thinking about? This question is not within your competence. It is concerned with the other world." Hence the law is despised. Mortals overbold! You breathe the breath of life, and yet do not believe that you must submit to the laws! Your kingdom is of the other world, yet you throw this world into disorder. This is the manner in which Christianity has broken the unity of the State; this is the manner in which it has produced wars, which have torn asunder almost all the kingdoms of Europe. You say that politics have taken an important share in this. I agree to this. But what follows? Is it not a danger for a State that ambitious persons should be able to find a pretext for throwing it into confusion? The spirit of the Christian constitution, far from strengthening the State, has done nothing but weaken it, by shattering the unity of government and in providing powerful pretexts for giving colour to the proceedings of ambitious persons. But the arguments by which you support your views are amusing. With an air of triumph, you ask why Protestant Switzerland, French and Piedmontese Calvinists have not been disturbed by civil dissensions. Why? Because they have a common enemy in the Papist. So long as Christians were persecuted by the pagan and kept in check, they were humble and good. The spirit of their constitution, which has since become manifest, was overlaid by their want of power. Political wars, the vigilance which was necessary to the nation in order that the sovereign might not attack what remained of their liberties, the existence of those who had been papists still in considerable numbers, the necessity which the Protestants of Germany had of being protected against the Papal leagues, were all motives which preserved the Swedes from religious wars. But we cannot open the annals of Europe without finding many other evils which owe their origin to the different reformed sects.

If you desired to point out the errors into which Jean Jacques has fallen, you ought to have read him first. You interpret his words literally when he says that the idea of a kingdom of the other world could never enter into the head of a pagan; that is to say, that they could never conceive that men could come together and form a society solely from religious motives. They knew the human heart but too well, not to see clearly that this would tend to the destruction both of their religion and their government, and that these Christians would one day be despotic masters of the world, whatever they might say to the contrary. The absurdity of what you say on page 26 is such that the best way of refuting it is to read your own scheme. Do we wait till the city is in a blaze before we arrest the incendiaries? Besides, you do not understand that it was impossible to prove the results of the Christian constitution because by its nature it is not developed till it has the mastery. Undoubtedly they were weak because they were dispersed, they were deficient in union and energy because their constitution was not yet completed. The energy which is required to repel by force the sovereign who attacks you and whom you are accustomed to obey is very different from the passion which inspires the enthusiasm of martyrdom. One is a sign of greatness of soul, the other of fanaticism. If an emperor cannot become a Christian, or Christianity become prosperous without all the springs of government being broken, it is clear that this religion can give no assistance to government, and that, on the contrary, by its speedy corruption it can only cause infinite injury to society.

Is this apparent in ancient religions? Certainly not. All you can say is that the corruption of religion corresponds to the corruption of the government. If you reflect upon the constitution of Christianity you will discover in it the origin of wars, and, I would venture to say, the little respect we have for religion. You confess that you do not understand how the clergy can be master and legislator in their own country. Do you believe that you will induce us to suspect that Rousseau had no clear idea before him when he used these words? On the contrary, you induce us to believe that it would have been better for you if you had never written a line. Wherever the clergy form a corporation which belongs to several states they are masters, inasmuch as its decisions are independent of all the other bodies of the State. It is a legislator, inasmuch as it has authority over consciences. In short, whatever it does it does despotically.

We have now examined the reasons which M. de Roustan gives in order to prove that Christianity did not in any way destroy the unity of the State, and was not the cause of wars which have disturbed Christian States. The next question which we have to examine is whether Christianity tends to weaken the tie between citizens and the country to which they belong. Rousseau gives reasons to show that it does. M. de Roustan begins by relying for support on the authority of Montesquieu, who not only decides nothing, but is even opposed to him. Everything that he says from pp. 42 to 44 is entirely in favour of the opinions of Jean Jacques, or, to speak more correctly, is absolutely useless. He desires to justify Christianity. But who is attacking it in the sense in which he defends it? For the question to determine is, not whether Christ did good or harm, but simply whether Christianity tends to detach a citizen from his country.

"As slaves had lost their liberty, all that remained was to prevent their further degeneration, and as they could not combine to love each other as fellow-citizens, to teach them to love each other as human beings." If the object of the gospel was to discipline slaves, the controversy is at an end. If they learnt that they could "still deserve respect by dying for moral liberty, as they before acquired immortality by dying for political liberty," it is evident that in their souls one desire was substituted for another, and good-bye to fatherland. "If they learnt that their haughty tyrants, whose power was only limited by their caprice, enjoyed a glory which was only a flash of lightning and a power which was only weakness; that a God, in whose sight they were but crawling worms, watched minutely over their whole conduct; that death awaited His commands, death which would bring them before His tribunal to receive the rewards or punishments which their administration of government deserved;"—they drew the inference that a tyrant was given them by God, that punishment belonged to Him alone who had placed the tyrant in his position. Goodbye to the respect for its own existence which is so necessary to a government. Should we expect M. de Roustan to tell us after this that "the Christian religion prepared nations to recover their political liberty if they found an opportunity of doing so? A nation which is endowed with morality and a spirit of unity, needs only the will to shake off the yoke to be able to do so." But you told us that the object of the gospel was to discipline slaves. If this was its object, it would have been very foolish to give them the energy and inspire them with the wish to shake off the yoke of the sovereign. What astounding contradictions! But let us examine your principle. "A nation," you say, "which is endowed with morality and a spirit of unity needs only the will to shake off the yoke to be able to do so." Christians united! Do not say this? Christians can never be divided. Tranquillity is the essence of religion, but political unity is a passionate sentiment which little suits the cold pyrrhonism of Christianity. Even if we admitted your principle the will would always be wanting, for as soon as the will appeared (it would cease to exist). Not only is it necessary for the unity of the State that it should contain neither corporations nor individuals who can interfere with the methods which it uses to arrive at the end of government, but it is also necessary that the sentiments which are inspired by the different institutions should tend to the same end. But surely Christianity inspires us with a marked indifference for all actions which are purely human.

It is true that Christianity tends to make us happy. The object of government should be also to make us happy. But it does not follow from this that Christianity does not destroy the unity of the State. They arrive at the same end by paths which are entirely opposed, and indeed inconsistent with each other. Christianity makes us happy by making us consider all the evil which we experience as a punishment from God which will be recompensed in another life. It says, this life is made happy by the hope of a future life. The object of government, on the other hand, is to assist the weak against the strong, and by these means to make every one enjoy a sweet tranquillity which leads to happiness. Besides, since the ministers of law are not at the same time ministers of religion, it results that the religious body has a character of its own, and this character is all the stronger because its empire is purely metaphysical. The heart of a citizen, therefore, is divided between the ministers of the law and those of religion. Now, the natural tendency of man is the desire of domination. A corporation which is all-powerful without real power would naturally desire to have real power. And this is what results. I affirm that Christianity destroys the unity of the State because there exists a corporation which has a spirit of its own, independent of the spirit of the State. I mean the Jesuits.

But you admit yourself that Jesus says to men that God is the first of kings, and that they must not obey unjust orders. In this way you make the subject judge of the actions of his sovereign. Conscience, you say, will form this tribunal. But by whom is conscience controlled? By the ministers of religion. You see, that is the way the unity of the State is destroyed.

You assert that it would have been better for pagan monarchs if this principle had been received. I am quite willing to believe it. Christianity may have softened manners, but that has no connection with the matter before us.

But do you not see that what you tell me on behalf of the Vicomte d'Orthe is of a very different nature in paganism or in some other religion? In that case unity would exist because there is only one body which is concerned with the matter, but with us the ministers of religion consider themselves as authorized to protect it, or at least to applaud it. Whether this is good or bad has nothing to do with the question. But you admit what you desire to deny, because you say by implication that the priests would be ready to induce the people to revolt against unjust orders whilst you say that the prince can avoid this difficulty by choosing virtuous priests. This is beside the question. I will, however, show you how you contradict yourself. You say that Jesus gave advice that an unjust order should not be obeyed. The more virtuous a minister of religion is the more he will follow the maxims of Jesus Christ. I mean by a rebel a man who does not obey the orders of his sovereign.

You tell us that the emperors made a great mistake by enriching the priests, but you do not see that this was a natural consequence, first, of the power which they had over the conscience of the prince, and secondly, of the good or harm which they could effect in the State. What! you would prevent a man or a corporation who is more powerful than any one else from being rich? Penetrate a little into the human heart; you will find that the wealth of the clergy was a natural consequence of its determination not to be dependent upon the government, and consequently ought to be laid to the account of Christianity as well as the abuses and war which it has caused. I speak of its being independent of the government. This is obvious. Being independent on the spiritual side, it must necessarily have some influence on the temporal side.

The Gospels say, "Obey your sovereign." What meaning have these words for me? I do not regard them, but the secret springs and the constitutions of the society which say just the opposite. They may say, "Remain poor and virtuous," but the springs of their institution say, "Be rich." But if we follow strictly the spirit of Christianity, the unity of the State is broken. This is proved both by this reason, and by the consequences of the spirit of the constitutions. Rousseau was quite right in saying that the doctrine of Jesus caused intestine divisions which have never ceased to disturb the Christian world. These suspicions of heresy surely follow from the intolerance and pedantry of Christianity. Did Paganism produce any similar result? It is of no importance whether the Churches were conducted in a Christian manner or not, if it is allowed that these wars were consequent upon the constitution of Christians. This is all I need for my argument. It is just on this point that Rousseau says that, unity being broken, civil wars have ensued because they were authorized by ministers of religion. But it seems that you have not understood Rousseau. He does not say that it is the gospel which directly occasions these abuses, but what follows from the abuses of the political constitution of Christianity. But let us suppose that Rousseau had really said that the gospel inspires discord. The argument which you bring against him is amusing. Despotism always changes into tyranny: does it follow from this that certain good sovereigns cannot make their subjects happy? Switzerland was not disturbed by internal wars, because it had to fight against the Roman Catholics, and because of the small size of each canton, which is a result of the Helvetic constitution. The Protestants of Sweden, Denmark, and France did not make war amongst themselves, because they had to contend against the Roman Catholics.

But why, I ask you, do you rather defend the Protestants of the Confession of Augsburg than the Roman Catholic Christians? Neither of the two parties would recognize you as a champion.

Notwithstanding the title of "friend" which you give to Rousseau, you are not fitted to read his works. In order to prove that the pagans might have had the idea of a kingdom of another world, you tell us … by which I infer that you do not understand what Rousseau wishes to say. The statesmen and sovereigns of paganism would never believe that the Christians spoke sincerely, but that they would never be contented with a metaphysical empire. It is obvious from this that their work is hidden behind a deep political wisdom. You say that the pagans ought to have waited until the Christians had shown their hand. Suppose now an army were to enter your town, but had not as yet manifested any hostile design....

D

A MEETING IN THE PALAIS-ROYAL

Paris, Thursday, November 22, 1787.
Hôtel de Cherbourg, Rue de Four, Saint-Honoré.

I had just come out of the Italian Opera, and was walking at a good pace in the alleys of the Palais-Royal. My spirit, stirred by the feelings of vigour which are natural to it, was indifferent to the cold; but when once my mind became chilled, I felt the severity of the weather, and took refuge in the galleries. I was just entering the iron gates, when my eyes became fixed on a person of the other sex. The time of night, her figure, and her youth, left me no doubt as to what her occupation was. I looked at her; she stopped, not with the impudent air common to her class, but with a manner which was quite in harmony with the charm of her appearance. This struck me. Her timidity encouraged me, and I spoke to her. I spoke to her; I, who, more sensible than any one of the horror of her condition, have always felt stained by even a look from such a person! But her pallor, her frail form, ber soft voice, left me not a moment in suspense. I said to myself, "Either this woman will serve me for the observation which I wish to make, or she is a mere senseless object."

"You are very cold," I said; "how can you think of going out into the garden?"

"Ah, sir! hope encourages me; I must close my evening." She said these words with such indifference, and with so little emotion, that I was touched, and went into the garden with her.

"You seem to have a very weak constitution; I am astonished that you are not tired of your trade?"

"Ah, sir! one must do something."

"Perhaps; but is there no occupation more suited to your health?"

"No, sir; one must live."

I was charmed; I saw that she at least gave me an answer, a success which I had never met with before.

"You must come from the North, for you do not mind the cold?"

"I come from Nantes, in Brittany."

"I know that part of the world. Would you mind telling me how you lost your virtue?"

"An officer ruined me."

"Are you sorry for it?"

"Yes, very." Her voice here took a tone and a tenderness, which I had not before noticed. "Very. My sister is now in a good position; why could not I have been so as well?"

"How did you come to Paris?"

"The officer who ruined me, whom I detest, abandoned me. I had to fly from my mother's anger. Another officer came, took me to Paris, abandoned me; and a third, with whom I have just been living three years, succeeded him. Although a Frenchman, business summoned him to London, and he is there now."

"Let us go to your rooms."

"But what shall we do there?"

"Well, we will warm ourselves, and you shall satisfy your desire."

I was far from becoming scrupulous; I had provoked her, so that she might not run away when she felt herself pressed by the arguments which I was preparing for her, by pretending a morality which I wished to prove that I did not possess... .

THE MEMOIRS OF BOURRIENNE

The first of the ten volumes of Bourrienne's *Memoirs of Napoleon* is the principal source from which the stories of his youth, which appear in the ordinary biographies, have been taken. These memoirs, published 1829-1830, when Bourrienne was eighty years old, were arranged and edited by Villemarest, who is greatly responsible for them. Immediately after their appearance they roused a storm of remonstrance from some of those who had known Napoleon best—Gourgaud, Meneval, Davout, Cambacérès, and others. These are collected in a book entitled *Bourrienne et ses erreurs volontaires et involontaires*, and published in two volumes. Few, if any, of these corrections concern the boyhood of Napoleon, but their existence throws discredit upon the whole of Bourrienne's testimony. O'Meara, in a pamphlet published in 1831, says of this work

"A perusal of these volumes, to which I would earnestly refer the public, will, I have no doubt, convince the most incredulous, that the memoirs of M. de Bourrienne have been proved, by incontrovertible evidence, to contain innumerable misrepresentations, either concocted through deliberate malice, or (which is equally probable) through absolute ignorance of transactions, many of which he pretends to have personally witnessed; that they teem with various falsifications and fabulous conversations, in order to substantiate the assertions of their author; and that they are altogether so replete with contradictions and anachronisms, as to induce a belief that he merely got together a few noted documents and recollections from a well-known manufacturer of memoirs in Paris, the proprietors of which are partly booksellers and partly literary men-of-all-work, who are ever on the alert to contract with anyone having had opportunities of being near the person of Napoleon, requiring, however, no more than permission to use his name as an authority for a mass of anecdotical matter, which they undertake to supply from their own manufactory."

The most important sources of the history of Napoleon at Brienne are two in number: (1) *True Account of the Early Years of Bonaparte at the Military School at Brienne*, by M. C. H., one of his schoolfellows (London, 1797); and (2) *Traits caracteristiques de la jeunesse de Bonaparte et répetitions de différentes anecdotes qui ont été publiées à ce sujet* (Leipzig, 1802). The author of the first is an emigré who came to the school some fifteen or eighteen months after Bonaparte. He is supposed to have been one Cumming of Craigmillar, whose father was in the service of Prince Xavier of Saxony. The narrative is authentic, and bears every trace of truth. The second book is far less trustworthy; but the author may have been at Brienne, and have given a fairly true account of what happened at that school. It was consulted by Las Cases.

Villemarest, in compiling the memoirs of Bourrienne, has made much use of these two books. Bourrienne tells us that he was very intimate with Napoleon at Brienne. This was certainly not the case, although they were of the same age. It was to Bourrienne's advantage to lay claim to this intimacy in after life. The result is that what is true in Bourrienne's schooldays is taken from the other authorities above mentioned, and what is not taken from these authorities is generally not true. It is scarcely worthwhile to recount the minute details in which Bourrienne has gone wrong. To sum up in the words of M. Chuquet, "Can we henceforth trust the so-called memoirs of Bourrienne? No! but we must read them, and while reading them with caution we shall find

something worth knowing and learning." Bourrienne was paid to supply some original documents besides his name, and he must have done so; and the skilful and intelligent Villemarest has, on his side, collected some authentic documents, for instance, the letter of Charles Bonaparte to Ségur, the notes of Madame Bourrienne on Bonaparte in 1795, the report on the 13th Vendémiaire, and others.

THE WRITINGS OF NAPOLEON

The writings of Napoleon, of which an account is given in the Introduction to this work, are, as enumerated by M. Masson, sixty in number, not counting the Souper de Beaucaire. Of these the first two, on Corsica and on Suicide, are printed in Appendix I. The third, dated 9 May 1796, written like the other two, at Valence, is a very remarkable production for a young man of seventeen. It is a reply to the defence of Christianity written by M. A. J. Roustan, a Geneva minister, and published at Amsterdam. M. Roustan's book is intended specially to be an answer to Book IV, Chapter VIII, of the *Contrat Social*, by Rousseau. Bonaparte's paper is unfinished, obviously thrown off at a single effort by someone who is not perfectly familiar with the French language, but is so interesting in itself, and as foreshadowing the ecclesiastical policy of the future Emperor, that it has been thought well to print it in its entirety. The fourth paper is an account of a meeting in the Palais Royal, dated Paris, Thursday, 22 November 1787, which is also printed in Appendix I. The fifth, dated Paris, 27 November 1787 11 p.m., is a very short fragment of an Introduction to a History of Corsica. The sixth is a rather tedious parallel between the love of our country and the love of glory, crowded with historical allusions.

The seventh paper has a curious interest. It consists of an imaginary correspondence between King Theodore of Corsica and Horace Walpole, whom Bonaparte styles Milord Walpole. Baron Neuhof had been proclaimed King of Corsica in 1736, under the title of Theodore I, and had nearly succeeded in delivering the island from the tyranny of the Genoese. However, he was eventually confined in a London prison for debt, upon which Horace Walpole collected a subscription to assist him, and when he died in 1756, erected a monument to him in St Anne's, Soho, where it still exists.

Theodore writes to "Milord Walpole" from a London prison—

"Milord, why did you drag me from the obscurity in which I lived? I was groaning in a cell, but I was groaning unknown. My name and my rank were revealed to few; they were a secret to my friends, to my companions in slavery, and allowed me to taste the sad consolation of being revered by the criminals or the unhappy mortals who surrounded me. If their souls, oppressed by the horrors of their prison, formed plans for deliverance, I was the first to be told of it. There was not one who did not say, 'We will break our chains with you, and you shall be our head.'

But since the day, milord, when you caused them to know who I was, I have fallen to be the last in their estimation, and I am the object of their ridicule. How unjust are mankind! I desired to contribute to the happiness of a nation. I succeeded for a moment, and you esteemed me. Destiny has changed. I am in a prison, and you despise me."

Milord to Theodore—

"You suffer and you are unhappy. These are two good reasons for laying claim to the pity of an Englishman. Come forth from your prison and receive a pension of three thousand pounds for your support."

It has been remarked that the idealization of English generosity which is presented in Walpole's letter may have led Napoleon to trust the English at Rochefort, in 1815, so unhappily for himself.

The next batch of Bonaparte's writings contains the numbers from eight to thirty-five inclusive. They were written at Auxonne, between June, 1788, and September, 1789, from the age of eighteen to that of twenty. Six of them are purely military. There are the Constitution of the Calotte, mentioned earlier. It is interesting and amusing, but too long to be inserted. There follow five papers on various subjects connected with artillery, which may still be of interest to military men. The fourteenth paper contains some notes on the Republic of Plato. Bonaparte seems to have been struck by the definition of justice—"to render everyone his due." He seems to have studied Plato in the translation of the Abbé Grau. Madame de Rémusat tells us that Napoleon frequently conversed on the subject of Plato. Then follow some notes on the government and religion of the ancient Persians, taken from Rollin, and on the geography and history of Greece, drawn from the same source. The following remarks on the government of Athens seem to be original, and have nothing to do with Rollin—

"The first King is always the first man of his nation. The reasons which raised him above his equals ought to keep him in his position, and his authority has always been more absolute than that of his successors, until corruption, introducing into the government religion preached by venal men, at length caused men to forget their dignity and the final reasons for the institution of all governments. Then despotism raised its hideous head, and man, becoming degraded, losing his liberty and his energy, felt in himself nothing but depraved tastes. The torrent once overflowing its banks, nothing can stop it, and we see existing side by side men who have nothing to eat, and those who consume the existence of a thousand families. The government of a Caligula, a Claudius, a Nero, is possible because the class which is interested in supporting the government has been able to deprive the wretched people who are the victims of it, even of the desire to rid themselves of it. How can the Creator have permitted the disfigurement of His work to this extent?" Then follow remarks on Lacedemonia, Thrace, the Scythians, Magna Grecia, and general Greek history, mainly drawn from Rollin.

The sixteenth paper is a manuscript of eighteen folio pages on Ancient History, also based on Rollin. The remarks on Hannibal are interesting "The only reasons which caused Hannibal to fail and put an end to his brilliant success in Italy was the want of reinforcements. He left Carthage with 100,000 men and 40 elephants; when he arrived at the Pyrenees, he left Hanno behind him with 15,000 men, and sent the same number back to Carthage, so that when he had crossed the mountains he had only 50,000 men and 9,000 horses. He had 400 leagues to travel before he reached Italy. He had to subdue several hostile tribes in Spain, to pass the Pyrenees, to cross the Rhone, and to scale the Alps. He did this in five months and a half. He spent a fortnight in crossing the Alps, and arrived on the banks of the Po in the month of September. By this time his army was reduced to 20,000 infantry and 6,000 horses. At the battle of Cannæ, Hannibal had 40,000 men and 10,000 horses, part of which were from Gaul. Four thousand of these were killed, as well as 11,500 of his old soldiers, and 200 horses, whilst the Romans, who had 86,000 men, lost 70,000 and more than 10,000 prisoners. How then could Hannibal, with the 26,000 miserable men which remained to him, hope to capture Rome? Nevertheless, with an army so inferior in numbers he held his own against the whole of the Roman forces, and he always had opposed to him two armies which changed every year. He received nothing from Carthage, neither money, nor elephants, nor soldiers. He died in exile from his country, betrayed by King Prusias, to whom he had rendered the greatest service, by enabling him to gain victories over his enemies. When Prusias, King of Bithynia, wished to deliver him up to Flaminius, a man of consular rank, whom the Romans had deputed for that purpose, Hannibal died of poison, in the year 182 B.C., at the age of 70."

The paper concludes with an account of Assyria.

The seventeenth manuscript consists of notes taken from the work of Abbé Raynal—"The philosophical and political history of European establishments and commerce in the two Indies." The eighteenth contains notes on the History of England from the earliest times to the peace of 1763. It is very long, and consists of seventy-four printed pages in Masson's work. The notes are taken from a History of England by John Barrow, which is now but little known or esteemed. We learn from these notes the profound interest which Bonaparte took in the history and the constitution of England, and the deep study which he had given to them.

These notes have been translated with copious annotations by Mr. H. F. Hall, and were published in 1905. Added to these is a short notice of an English novel on the Earl of Essex, the author of which is unknown. It contains a harrowing account of a dream of the Countess of Essex, who saw her husband coming to her with his throat cut, calling out, "Jane Betsy, Jane Betsy! dear Jane! Jane, you have forgotten me! thou sleepest, but touch!"

The twentieth manuscript contains notes on Frederick the Great from an unknown source. This does not contain anything of interest. Next, in January, 1789, the memoirs of the Baron de Tott on the Turks and Tartars receive attention. Then follow, written in the same month, notes on the essay on "Lettres de Cachet," by Mirabeau. Eighteen pages of Masson's text are occupied by extracts from the "Espion Anglais," the English spy, a secret correspondence between Milord All-Eye and All-Ear, published in London, 1784. The twenty-sixth manuscript is devoted to Natural History, drawn mainly from Buffon. Great attention is paid to different theories of generation and the development of the embryo, and kindred subjects.

The twenty-seventh manuscript consists of extracts from the "History of the Arabs under the Government of the Caliphs," by the Abbé de Marigny. There follows a short account of the "Masked Prophet," in four folio pages, which has been published both by Libri and Jung. The first four paragraphs will give an idea of the composition—

"In the year 160 of the Hegira, Mahadi reigned at Baghdad. This prince, grave, generous, and enlightened, saw the Arab Empire prosper in the bosom of peace. Feared and respected by his neighbours, he employed himself in fostering the progress of science, when his power was disturbed by Hakem, who, from the recesses of Kharassan, began to make disciples in all parts of the Empire. Hakem, of lofty stature, gifted with a manly and vigorous eloquence, called him the Messenger of God; he preached a purer morality which pleased the multitudes. Equality in rank and fortune was the main text of his sermons. The people collected under his banner; Hakem had an army.

The Caliph and his nobles felt the necessity of stifling so dangerous an innovation in its birth, but their troops were beaten more than once, and Hakem gained every day a new preponderance.

Nevertheless, a cruel malady, the result of the fatigues of war, began to disfigure the face of the prophet. He was no longer the most beautiful of the Arabs; his proud and noble features, his large and fiery eyes were disfigured. Hakem became blind. This change might have slackened the enthusiasm of his partisans, he therefore determined to wear a silver masque.

He showed himself amongst his followers. Hakem still retained all his eloquence. His address had the same effect. He spoke to them, and convinced them that he only carried the masque in order to prevent mankind from being dazzled by the light which proceeded from his face."

Bonaparte then proceeds to recite the well-known story how the Veiled Prophet, being defeated by the Caliph, poisoned himself and his followers, leaving his concubine alone to receive the conquerors on their approach.

The twenty-ninth paper is concerned with the constitution of the Venetian Republic, a matter which became of great interest to Napoleon some ten years later.

Much has been written upon the ideal education of a prince, but no prince ever received at the hands of his tutor so sound and complete an education in the science of government as Bonaparte when at Auxonne devised for himself. We do not know which to admire most, the vast range of study, the excellent choice of materials, the directness with which the heart of a subject is attacked, or the crisp, nervous language in which the notes are couched. It is interesting to see that the statesman outtops the warrior; the vicissitudes of men and of governments had more attraction for him, at the age of nineteen, than the explosion of gunpowder, or the course of a bullet from a rifled cannon.

When Bonaparte was in Corsica during the first five months of 1788, he conceived the idea of writing the history of that island, and collected materials for the purpose. He also formed the plan of writing some letters on Corsica, more as a patriot than as an historian. He intended at first to dedicate them to the minister Brienne, with whom he had special relations, and, after his fall, to Neckar. He submitted the letters when completed to his old teacher of French, the Père Dupuy, and we have his corrections. From these we may infer the style and turn of the composition, and we shall see that, intensely Corsican, they express a deep enthusiam for Paoli, and a hatred of the French who have conquered the island. These views were to give way at a later period to saner sentiments. Unfortunately, the letters themselves have disappeared without a trace. There are, however, two papers on Corsica which belong to this period. One is the commencement of a story, which deserves notice. An English translation of it appeared in the *Cosmopolitan*. The other is a letter to M. Giubega of Calvi, between whose family and the Napoleon family there existed intimate ties of friendship.

Bonaparte was in Corsica from September 1789 to February 1791. Two manuscripts belong to this period, numbered XXXVII and XXXVIII in Masson's collection. The first of these consists of three letters on Corsica addressed to the Abbé Raynal. They are extremely interesting, and contain a history of Corsica from the time of the Phocœan occupation to the year 1730, but are too long for translation in this place. The second is the letter to Buttafuoco, mentioned in the text. The greater part of the year 1791 was spent at Auxonne and at Valence.

Fourteen manuscripts belong to this period (Numbers XXXIX—LII). These are Impression de Voyage, notes on the History of the Sorbonne, taken from the work of the Abbé Duveonet, and extracts from Coxe's *Travels in Switzerland*. On 24 June at Valence he attacks Machiavelli's *History of Florence*, in a French translation.

Number XLVIII consists of an interesting fragment entitled "Republic or Monarchy." Massoa is of opinion that it was written in June, 1791, just after the flight of the King to Varennes—

"For a long time my taste has led me to give my attention to public affairs. If an unprejudiced publicist can have any doubts as to the preference which ought to be given to republicanism or monarchy, I think that today his doubts ought to be removed. Republicans are insulted, calumniated, and threatened, and the only reason given is that republicanism is impossible in France. Indeed, orators of monarchical opinions have largely contributed to the fall of the monarchy, for after having exhausted their breath in useless analyses, they end by saying that republican government is impossible because it is impossible. I have read all the speeches of the monarchical orators; I have seen their powerful efforts to support a bad cause. They make vague assertions which they do not prove. In fact, if I had any doubts, the reading of these speeches would have removed them.

"They say, 'Twenty-five millions of people cannot live under a republic. With morality no republic! A great nation must have a centre of union.'

To say that twenty-five millions of men cannot live under a republic is a maxim which is opposed to sound principles of polity."

The forty-ninth manuscript is also extremely interesting. It is a dialogue between Bonaparte and his bosom friend Des Mazis on the subject of love. It opens thus—

"De Mazis: 'What, sir! do you ask me what love is? Are you not made of the same stuff as other men?'

"Bonaparte: 'I do not ask you for a definition of love. I was once in love myself, and I remember it well enough not to require those metaphysical developments, which only confuse matters. I go further than denying its existence. I believe it to be injurious to society, to the individual happiness of mankind; in short, I think that love does an infinity of mischief, and that it would be a kindly scheme for some protecting divinity to deliver both ourselves and the world of its existence.'"

De Mazis goes on to place his love of Adelaide above the political and historical studies of his friend, but Bonaparte naturally gives himself the best of the argument.

The fifty-second manuscript contains the "Discours de Lyon," of which an account has been given in the text. Preceding this are some reflections on the state of nature, and some notes from the Lyons essay.

The remaining eight manuscripts are purely on military matters, and then comes the Souper de Beaucaire, which is fully described in the text, Chapter XII.

No one can read these documents without great interest and profound emotion. We see the powerful and passionate mind of the young Bonaparte, swayed with every mood of feeling about the public affairs which interested him. As Burke says, "He was born a public creature;" and neither the false rhetoric which sometimes disfigures his style, or the private antipathies which sometimes warp his judgment, affect the corner-stone of majestic common sense and direct vision which is the foundation of his character. We find his eye fixed from the first on the government of men, on the relations of Church and State, and on the conditions most favourable to civilization and progress. He reads eagerly every book that he can find which may assist his preparation for the task which he instinctively knew lay before him. It is no light matter that he gives more space to the history of England than to that of any other country. It is his country of preference—that which he most admires and would most like to imitate. His notes are very instructive. They go direct to the point, and are interspersed with original remarks of the highest value. Bonaparte probably never forgot anything which he had read, and there is no reading indicated in his notes which would not be useful to him at some period in his career. Very interesting also is the sentimental side of his nature; his feeling for poetry, his family affection, and the yearning towards love, which he would have liked to encourage if he had not felt himself called to destinies which demanded the sacrifice of himself. Some day, perhaps, a convenient edition of these works will be published; until that time arrives. this essay will serve as an introduction to them.

APPENDIX IV

ORIGINAL DOCUMENTS FROM THE BRITISH MUSEUM CONCERNING THE SIEGE AND EVACUATION OF TOULON

I

Toulon, 1st Decr 1793.

The Enemy had established a Battery on the Green-hill or hauteur d'Arcines near Malbusquet which distress'd that Fort so much, General O'Hara determined to make a sortie, for the purpose of distroying it, or removing them, and as far as I can judge made a masterly disposition for that purpose. A body of between 3 and 4 Thousand Men under the Command of General Dundas passed the new river by the bridge on the old road to Olioulles. The Enemy were on their Guard, and soon fired their alarm beacons, notwithstanding which the Troops, under the cover of a heavy fire of Artillery, ascended the Hill in three columns and took possession of the Enemy's Battery with the loss of one Man killed and two wounded, and took an Officer with 25 Men Prisoners, but am sorry to add that such was the want of dicipline in our Troops and so much impetuosity, that the Royals or 1st Reg^t set up the Cry of Tallioh for Olioulles and push'd on through two more of the Enemy's Camps—The Spaniards and Neapolitans follow'd them, but could not resist their inclination and stop'd to plunder the Camps—the Royals still passed on and took another Battery of 2 Pieces of Cannon; just as they were yokeing the horses to bring them off they were attacked by the Enemy's whole Force of 5 or 6 Thousand Men, on which they abandoned the Guns with the loss of 6 Officers and 120 Men. The Enemy pursued them closely, and with little resistance on our part and seldom so many as five men seen together, and followed them into the first Battery in the hauteur d'Arcines, where unfortunately General O'Hara had arrived—and was giving directions for removing the Guns, and where there was only 250 Piedmontois who did their best [but] found it impossible to recover the confusion that had taken place, and the whole became a scene of Rapin and Flight; in so much that the Guns were even left unspik'd in the Battery, General O'Hara was wounded and taken

148

Prisoner, and a Spanish Colonel Captain Snow killed; Capt. Reeves of the Royals wounded; Major Cambell of the 69th Regt missing most all our Artillery Officers wounded; The Royal Irish or 18th Regt lost 40 Men, the Loyal Louis between 40 and 50. Thus a Glorious Morning was lost by the Impetuosity of the Men, and the Youth of the Officers, The purpose of the Sortie was completely acquired if they had stop'd there. Capt. Reeves of the Royals is since dead.

II

Translation of a Letter from Toulon,
2nd December, 1793

No doubt you will hear very different reports relative to the Action which happened on the 30th Ult. in which the Governor who commanded the Troops was unfortunately taken Prisoner by the Republican Army.

This is the fact; the Republicans had erected a Battery near the Fort called Malbusque which would have greatly annoyed it, and it was resolved on the 30th Inst. to attack it; for this purpose about 2,400 Men went out at 4 O'Clock in the Morning under the Command of General O'Hara who attacked the Fort with success and carried it with little loss; the Battery consisted of 7 24Prs 2 Howitzers and 2 Mortars.

General O'Hara thought proper to pursue the Enemy who were soon dispersed, but the Environs of Toulon have numberless small hills and narrow vales which prevented the seeing a Column of 8,000 Republicans who were advancing to retake the Battery and it was impossible to oppose any resistance there being no Corps de Reserve, thus was the Battery retaken the General after being wounded in the Arm was made Prisoner as also several other Officers.

This unfortunate Affair has cost about 80 Men killed 150 Wounded and 20 made Prisoners. Their loss is said to be from 1,000 to 1,200 Men and 40 Prisoners. Several Flags of Truce have been received relative to the General but it is not believed the Republicans will take on themselves to exchange him.

III

Captn John Lucchesi, Commander of a Neapolitan Brigantine, *Ferdinand IV* from Toulon in 5 days, Deposeth, That on the 17th Inst. a General Attack was made by the French on the Advanced Posts and Forts, and particularly on Fort Balaguae, of which they became Masters owing to the Neapolitan Troops giving way. On the Morning of the 18th the English set fire to the Arsenals, and to several Ships of War, which produced a general Conflagration in the City. On the same day the Neapolitan Troops embarked with their Baggage on board the vessels of their own nation, and set sail immediately. The English and Spanish are still on shore, and remain in possession of Fort La Malgue. The English and Spanish Fleets with some French Ships were at Anchor out of the Reach of the Cannon of the Place, and all the other Transport Vessels were preparing to set out with French Royalists on board, who evacuated the City, by Permission from Lord Hood.

Leghorn, 22nd December, 1793.

Rt. Hon. Henry Dundas, Home Secretary,
to General O'Hara.

Whitehall, 20 December, 1793.

Sir,

Your Letter of the 13th November together with its inclosure, being a copy of a Letter from you to Lord Hood, have been duly received and laid before His Majesty.

I should have wished, along with that Letter, to have received a distinct return of the whole force, of every description, within the Town of Toulon, and likewise, so far as your information enables you to give it, an account of the probable amount and description of the Enemy's Force, by which you are opposed, for, without knowing these particulars, it is impossible to form any accurate judgment upon the subject of your letter. I have, however, the satisfaction to know that the mode of defending your position must have been maturely considered by you in the pains you have taken to investigate the various weak parts of the Fortress committed to your charge. Your being perfectly aware of the weak parts by which you are assailable, is the best proof I can receive that you are perfectly prepared to make the best use of your force to resist every hostile attack.

Notwithstanding the representation contained in your Letter to Lord Hood, and more generally referred to in your Letter to me, I confess I do not feel myself so much alarmed as I would otherwise be for the safety of Toulon, because, if I am not mistaken, the Force employed in the defence of that place amounts to near 17,000 men, and we have never yet learnt that the Force opposed to you has hitherto much exceeded that number. In making this observation, I am perfectly aware of what you state as to the want of discipline and military experience in a large proportion of the Troops which compose your Garrison, but this is a defect which must be daily wearing away, and I trust that, under your Conduct, and animated by the example and Exertions of the British Troops under your command, they will every day more and more become enabled to contribute to the substantial defence and safety of the place; and here I likewise derive considerable satisfaction from reflecting that the Troops by whom you are opposed are not probably the best disciplined or the most experienced in the operations of the Field, and I am confirmed in this opinion by reflecting on the very inferior exertions they have made in comparison with the Troops which have at different times been engaged with them, even after the Town of Toulon was put into our hands. I likewise perfectly attend to what you state respecting the disadvantages of the divided command which has hitherto prevailed at Toulon. I admit the inconvenience, and can only hope that, in consequence of the measures which have been taken, and the Instructions which you have received, that circumstance may in a great degree have been remedied, by the Spanish Commanders having acquiesced in the undoubted right we have claimed to the exclusive Command of the Town of Toulon, and likewise in the right to command the combined force assembled there, by virtue of your superior Rank to any held by the Spanish Generals. And I am sure I need not recommend to you the necessity of carrying on the Service with every degree of conciliation on your part that can conduce to preserve Cordiality amongst you.

Before closing my observations on the different points of difficulty in which you feel yourself placed in maintaining the defence of Toulon, I must again refer to a circumstance I have already adverted to; I mean the nature of the Enemy you are engaged with. It is natural for a Commanding Officer to be in the first place impressed with his own difficulties, and to be anxious that remedies may be supplied to obviate them. But every consideration of that kind is relative, and it is impossible for me to entertain a doubt that the Troops opposed to you are labouring under difficulties of a more serious nature than any that apply to your Garrison. The Rulers of France have found themselves pressed from different quarters during the last Campaign, and must of course have been obliged to draw away their best force to those places where the most powerful Armies were operating against them: It is therefore scarcely credible that any force they may have been able to collect at Toulon can be of a nature to entitle them to any great degree of pre-eminence on a comparison with those which form the Garrison of Toulon, and I must call your attention in a particular manner to a circumstance of the first consequence in all military operations and in which you have such an advantage, I mean the Article of Provisions. The Sea is open to you, it is shut to them, and considering the great difficulties they must be exposed to in that respect, and the immense exertions which they must make to supply their numerous Armies and Garrison Towns it is not unreasonable to suppose that any Army they have collected or may collect at Toulon, and which must of course be fed from the interior of France, must fight at great disadvantage against a Garrison plentifully supplied, and therefore relieved from that pressing danger to which besieged Towns are so often exposed.

I have endeavoured to lay these observations forcibly before you, and in considerable detail, in order to satisfy you on the grounds why your letter has not excited that degree of Alarm for the safety of Toulon which you may have supposed from the strong manner in which you have painted the difficulties of your situation. His Majesty has a perfect reliance on your vigourous exertions. He knows that nothing but extreme necessity will induce you to surrender a situation, the possession of which is so honourable to His Majesty's Arms, and so essential to the important cause in which he is engaged. Upon these considerations His Majesty selected you for the Government of Toulon, and he has a perfect reliance that your exertions operating with the force under your Command will be available to overcome every difficulty.

I have not dwelt upon it, but in observing upon the force under your Command, I cannot totally lay out of my view the Aid you are entitled to expect from the Inhabitants within the Town. It would appear that bodies of them might be employed to lessen the fatigues of the Garrison in some of the operations of defence. I am aware that many of them are not to be trusted, but this cannot apply to the great body of them, and considering the calamitous State to which a surrender of the place would reduce them, I cannot conceive but that with proper management great numbers of them may be induced to act, and afford material assistance.

But notwithstanding the Confidence His Majesty reposes in the exertions and resources I have stated, it is by no means His intention to overlook the difficulties you have stated, or to omit to obviate them by such additional force as He can spare from other pressing Services. It must be remembered that from the manner in which Toulon came into His Majesty's Possession it was impossible to be prepared with a force adequate to His wishes or to the importance of the acquisition: Every Exertion has since been made and will continue to be made. Since the date of your dispatch you will probably have received a large additional reinforcement from Gibraltar. The Aid of the Milanese Troops has been withheld much longer than was expected, but fresh and earnest requisitions on that subject have been made at the Court of Vienna, and I hope will be attended with speedy success. A negotiation is open for obtaining as speedily as possible such further reinforcements of Sardinian Troops as may make the whole Force of that Nation at Toulon amount to Ten or Twelve Thousand Men. And it is intended with all expedition to send for your further reinforcement the 23^d, the 35th, and the 40th

Regiments in addition to the other British Forces serving there. How far any further reinforcements can or ought to be sent must depend upon the nature and extent of the Service to be carried on from that quarter in the further progress of the War. Upon that Subject I will have occasion to write to you by some early conveyance in which I shall advert to that part of your Letter which expresses your opinion as to the inexpedience of acting offensively against the Enemy from that side of France.

Although from the contents of this letter you will be satisfied that the abandonment of Toulon is not an Event to which I look forward or expect to hear of, still considering the terms in which you have stated your Situation, I have thought it my duty to write to Lord Hood on the supposition of so improbable an Event. He will, agreable to his Instructions, communicate the Contents to you, and you will operate with his Lordship in the Execution of any Measures which such a Necessity might suggest.

I am, Sir,
Your most obedient humble Servant,

HENRY DUNDAS.

HEADNOTE.—This Letter was rec^d by Lieutenant-General Dundas, at Sea after the Evacuation of Toulon and the capture of General O'Hara.

Henry Dundas to Lieutenant-General Dundas

[Private]

London, 20th Dec^r, 1793.

My Dear Sir,

General Ohara will of course communicate to you my official letters in answer to the one I have received from him. I cannot however permit the Messenger to depart without mentioning to you that neither General Ohara's letter nor your private one were calculated to inspire us with either good spirits or much confidence in the exertions to be made at Toulon. The whole of the Correspondence seems calculated to point out every Difficulty in the World, but omits in any one Sentence to mention either your Measures to overcome those Difficulties, or what in truth you conceived would be the ultimate consequence of them. You must be aware that Toulon came into our hands at a moment when it was impossible for us to have made any preparations for such an event. That Defect was on the first emergency made up by the Spirited Exertions of a handfull of British troops aided by the native Gallantry and Spirits of the British Seamen supported by no other military force than a few thousands of Spanish troops which it is now the tone to consider as good for nothing. In this Situation we found ourselves before the arrival of our General Officers, and the Reinforcment of large Bodies of troops and the hopes of still more. But no sooner is this accomplished after the most vigorous Exertions that were I believe ever made in the same period of time than we are accosted with Dispatches which are little short of announcing the abandonment of the Place, and with scarce a Ray of hope held out to us. General Ohara was not compelled as a Matter of Duty to undertake this Service. He went to Toulon as a Volunteer, and to his surprise found himself appointed Governor of the Place; Under those Circumstances His Majesty has a right to expect as vigorous a Defence of the Town of Toulon as ever was given to any Place, and I make no doubt he will not be disappointed in that Expectation, but there is no occasion to enhance that merit by an exaggerated Statement of Difficulties, without his mentioning any one of the Circumstances which upon a Comparison of the Relative Situation of the Enemy and his own do certainly when analised considerably diminish the force of some of the apprehensions which have been held out. Nothing can be more proper than that Officers should fairly and candidly state all their Difficulties, but they are not to look for Impossibilities; We are entitled to some Credit in having it thought of us that we are not insensible to the Importance of Toulon, and of course do not require any *Stimulus* to induce us to give every additional force to it that other Services will admit of. In fact We have done so, and shall continue to do so, but let us in return receive at least the Satisfaction of being informed that our Exertions at home will be met with Exertions equal to them on the Spot.

There is one Circumstance I cannot omit more particularly to notice. Both in General Oharas publick letter and in your Private one I am led to suppose that the Defence of the Place would be easy or at least the Difficulty of defending it much less, if it was not for the Harbour and the Fleet being likewise necessary to be defended. But it is no where stated that the Harbour can be abandoned without giving up the communication by Sea, nor does it appear that you have ever in concert with Lord Hood taken the Subject under consideration so as to report to us whether the line of Defence can be so circumscribed, as that if the Fleets were removed from the Harbour, your Task of defending would be proportionably lessened. In no letter of Lord Hoods does he state that any such Proposition was stated to him or he called upon to consider it. Unless this had been done and the Result of such a Consultation fairly laid before us, it must on the smallest reflexion occur to you that the Statement of the Defence of the Place being encreased in Difficulty by the harbour and Fleet amounts to no more than a Repetition of the fact that you are in Difficulty, but without giving us the smallest information whether any Measure was in contemplation by the Removal of the Fleet or any other Circumstance which could tend to lessen your Difficulties.

Altho this letter is addrest to you, I do not mean that any part of it should be kept back from General Ohara. Nobody carries to a higher Pitch than I do the Propriety and endeed the Duty of Ministers to support the Character and Reputation of the officers they employ; I think We are even in honour bound to support their Errors and defend their Mistakes, but while I have the honour to serve his Majesty I will set my Face against the modern Practice of every Officer when he goes upon Service sitting down to make a Catalogue of Difficulties and Grievances, which never had nor never can have good effect upon any Service, and must always expose the Person doing so to the imputation of beginning his Services with preparatory apologies for its failure. I am no Soldier and therefore not entitled to form a judgement, but I can say with great confidence that such a train of thinking and acting would augur ill for Vigorous Exertions in Civil life.

I have not time at present to write to you on any other Subject, but I remain,
>My Dear Sir,
>>Yours sincerely,
>>>HENRY DUNDAS.

HEADNOTE.—To Lieutenant-General Dundas from Secretary of State, received after the evacuation of Toulon, January, 1794.

Henry Dundas to Lieutenant- General Dundas.

[Private]

>>>Wimbledon, 28 Dec^r.

My Dear Sir,

I most sincerely hope your health will enable you to hold the situation which has dropt into your hands. We are doing what we can to give you relief and aid but it is scarcely possible to find any officers senior to you, and none of the Major General list we think can be found that are not already on Service. General Garth has been suggested, but to tell you the truth I objected to it on the ground of his having left the West Indies in so improper and unmilitary a Way. The present Idea is to send an officer of very high rank with the view of combating more effectually the Pretensions of the Spanish officers. The only officer of Service of that Description, (exclusive of those who have already declined Service) is Sir Henry Clinton. I have sent to him to know his Inclinations, and if He accepts he will of course be permitted to point out whom he wishes to serve under him, and

We will pay attention to his recommendation. If he has no particular suggestion to make We propose sending out Major General Alured Clarke, Charles Stuart and Balfour. If this arrangement takes place, I shall propose to the King to give you a Discretionary Power to remain or come as you please, and if your determination shall be to come home We must endeavour to keep a Place open for you in Flanders. But if things have taken a favourable turn with you perhaps with so much assistance, you may chuse to remain where you are.

Your last affair has given us great Concern and certainly very great apprehensions for the Place. As you are silent as to all the officers high and Low I cannot help entertaining my own Suspicions that the Rashness was not merely of the common soldiers. But as you have not told me your observations I shall keep my suspicions to myself. We have a report that you have since had a success at Cape Brun. The delay of the Austrians to send their promised 5,000 Men has put us out of all temper, but not so much as that of Sir Robert Boyd in keeping back the troops he was ordered to send. If things are all still safe, I hope the Reinforcement of Piedmontese which we understand you have got, with the additional troops from Gibraltar, and the 5,000 Austrians at last agreed to as you will see by the official Dispatch which comes with this, will put you much at your ease.

I have nothing further to detain you with,

Ever yours,
HENRY DUNDAS.

Lieutenant-General Dundas.

Henry Dundas to Lieutenant-General Dundas.

[Private]

Whitehall, 8 March, 1794.

My Dear David,

My long silence must have surprised you. The fact is that for near two months we have been in the daily intention of sending dispatches to the Mediterranean, but partly from the fluctuation of embarassing circumstances which have arisen at Genoa, and partly from the hopes of hearing further as to Your Measures respecting Corsica, we have postponed till now writing either to Lord Hood, Sir Gilbert Elliott, or Yourself. Even my present letter must be a very short one, for it would take a Ream of paper to write all I have to say to you. But I must write these few lines merely to say that You have given Yourself a great deal of unnecessary trouble in writing anything to me exculpatory of yourself for there is not one particle of your Conduct that has not merited and met with perfect approbation. If I have any doubts respecting any other quarter, I shall reserve them for future discussion, when we can do it freely, and with unreserved discussion. As to Lord Mulgrave, You do him injustice if you suppose that he has given any unfavorable impressions: In truth he has given me none at all, for I clearly saw on his first arrival here, that he had come home not in good humour. As nothing could be more unwarranted, I took no notice of it, but it certainly rather tended to keep back that freedom of communication which would otherwise have taken place.

In the first letter I had from You after the evacuation of Toulon, You expressed a Wish to be relieved from Your present Situation, and to be allowed leave to remain in Italy for the reestablishment of your health. I have taken no steps in consequence of that representation, for it soon appeared that there was a prospect of some operations, probably successful ones, against Corsica, and it would have been wrong under these circumstances to have sent out any person to supercede You. We hope soon to hear what has happened at Corsica, and when that is over, I shall then concert with Sir William Faucett what is best for You, and shall act accordingly.

In the mean time I remain,

My dear David,

Yours very sincerely,

HENRY DUNDAS.

Lieutenant-General Dundas.

[Sir David Dundas (1735-1820) did not become lieutenant-general till 1797; he became major-general in 1790. At Toulon he held brevet rank.]